James Carter

Songs of Work and Worship

A Collection of Hymns and Tunes for Devotional and Evangelistic Meetings

James Carter

Songs of Work and Worship
A Collection of Hymns and Tunes for Devotional and Evangelistic Meetings

ISBN/EAN: 9783337290078

Printed in Europe, USA, Canada, Australia, Japan

Cover: Foto ©Lupo / pixelio.de

More available books at **www.hansebooks.com**

SONGS OF WORK AND WORSHIP,

A Collection of Hymns and Tunes

FOR

Devotional and Evangelistic Meetings,

BY

JAMES CARTER.

A. S. BARNES & COMPANY,
NEW YORK.
1899.

PREFACE.

This Book is designed to serve the needs of the Church Prayer-meeting and the Evangelistic Services which form an increasingly important feature of modern Church methods, and also for the meetings of Young People's Societies. Its purpose is to afford expression for a buoyant, devoted Christian life in its needs and aspirations.

By the exclusion of lyrics appropriate to installations, dedications, funerals, corner-stone layings, Sabbath morning, and other services for which the larger Church Hymn-book must provide, it has been possible in a book of restricted size to include, in addition to the sterling and precious hymns needful for the social service, a large number of lyrics marked by a quicker movement and a pleasing refrain. Care has been exercised in the retention of favorite tunes, and in the introduction of new music of a popular character, yet of somewhat higher grade than much in common use. It is assumed that our churches will welcome a more classical style of music, if it be attractive and easily mastered.

The editor desires to express his thanks to Dr. G. L. Prentiss for permission to use hymn 133, to Dr. Rossiter W. Raymond for hymn 138, to the family of Dr. Charles S. Robinson for hymn 158, to Mrs. Frank G. Mason for hymn 255, and to J. M. Black, Esq. for permission to use hymn and tune 241. He desires also to thank Dr. H. R. Palmer, Dr. J. E. Rankin, and the Century Company, for permission to use their copyright tunes.

JAMES CARTER.

THE MANSE,
CHURCH OF THE COVENANT,
WILLIAMSPORT, PA.

CONTENTS.

	HYMNS
OPENING	1–4
EVENING	5–22
PRAYER	23–28
THE SCRIPTURES	29–30
GOD.—The Father	31–40
The Son.—Birth	42–47
Life	48–53
Death	54–56
Resurrection	57–58
Exaltation	59–62
The Holy Spirit	63–71
SALVATION.—Plan	72–77
Invitation	78–98
Acceptance	99–119
THE CHRISTIAN LIFE.—Love for Christ	120–129
Aspiration	130–133
Surety in Christ	134–141
Hardness and Solace	142–156
Pilgrimage	157–168
Warfare	169–191
Activity	192–208
Consecration	209–211
THE CHURCH.—Institutions and Fellowship	212–219
Baptism	220–221
The Lord's Supper	222–232
Missions	233–238
HEAVEN	239–253
TIMES, SEASONS, AND NATIONAL	254–262

	PAGES
ALPHABETICAL INDEX OF TUNES	154
METRICAL INDEX OF TUNES	155
INDEX OF AUTHORS AND TRANSLATORS	156–157
INDEX OF COMPOSERS AND HARMONIZERS	158–159
INDEX OF SUBJECTS	160–163
INDEX OF FIRST LINES	164–166

SONGS
OF
WORK AND WORSHIP.

1 NICÆA.   Rev. JOHN BACCHUS DYKES, 1861.

1. Holy, Holy, Holy! Lord God Almighty! Morn and noon and even our song shall rise to Thee; Holy, Holy, Holy, merciful and mighty! God in three persons, blessed Trinity!

2 Holy, Holy, Holy! all the saints adore Thee,
    Casting down their golden crowns around the glassy sea;
Cherubim and seraphim falling down before Thee,
    Which wert and art and evermore shalt be.

3 Holy, Holy, Holy! though the darkness hide Thee,
    Though the eye of sinful man Thy glory may not see;
Only Thou art holy; there is none beside Thee,
    Perfect in power, in love, and purity.

4 Holy, Holy, Holy! Lord God Almighty!
    All Thy works shall praise Thy name, in earth and sky and sea;
Holy, Holy, Holy, merciful and mighty;
    God in three persons, blessèd Trinity!

                        Bp. Reginald Heber, 1827. Sl. alt.

INVOCATION.

2 ITALIAN HYMN. 6. 6. 4. 6. 6. 6. 4.   FELICE GIARDINI, 1763.

1. Come, Thou almighty King, Help us Thy Name to sing, Help us to praise: Father! all glorious, O'er all victorious, Come, and reign over us, Ancient of days!

2 Come, Thou incarnate Word!
  Gird on Thy mighty sword;
    Our prayer attend;
  Come, and Thy people bless,
  And give Thy word success:
    Spirit of holiness!
      On us descend.

3 Come, holy Comforter!
  Thy sacred witness bear,
    In this glad hour:
  Thou, who almighty art,
  Now rule in every heart,
  And ne'er from us depart,
    Spirit of power!

4 To the great One in Three,
  The highest praises be,
    Hence evermore!
  His sovereign majesty
  May we in glory see,
  And to eternity
    Love and adore.

          Author Unknown, c. 1757.

GLORY (HUDSON). S. M.   Rev. RALPH HARRISON, 1784.

1. Come, we that love the Lord, And let our joys be known; Join in a song of sweet accord, And thus surround the throne.

MORN AND NOON AND EVE.

3 ORIENS. 8. 7. D. Rev. JAMES CARTER, 1894.

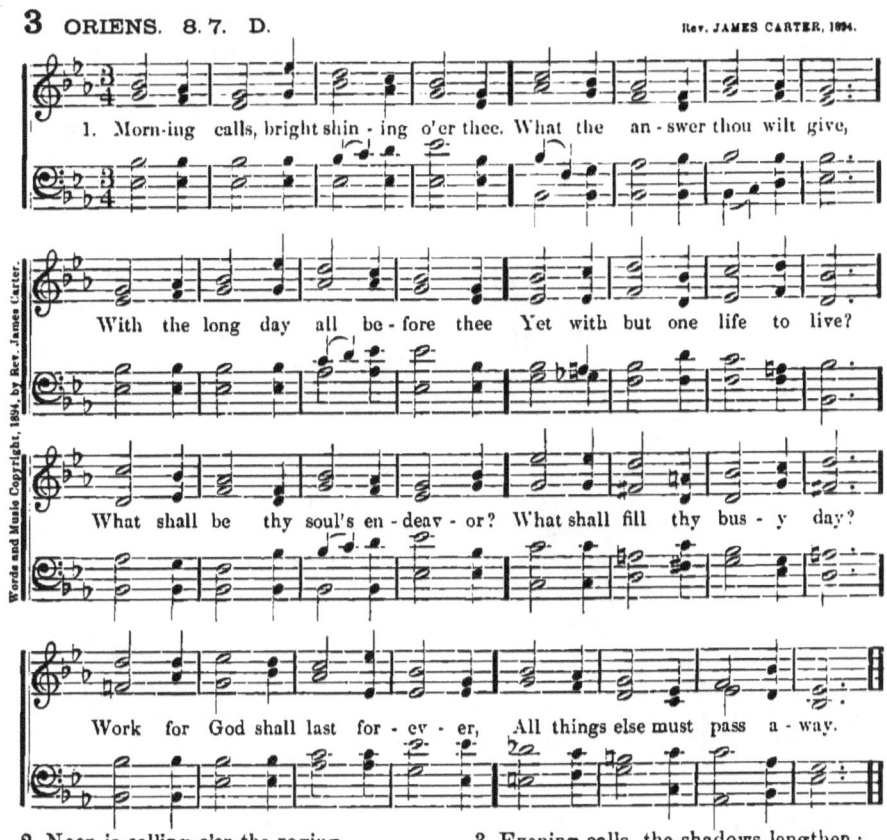

1. Morning calls, bright shining o'er thee. What the answer thou wilt give,
With the long day all before thee Yet with but one life to live?
What shall be thy soul's endeavor? What shall fill thy busy day?
Work for God shall last forever, All things else must pass away.

2 Noon is calling o'er the raging
  And the tumult of the strife.
What the warfare thou art waging?
  What the conflict of thy life?
Is it but for earth's promotion? [sweet,
  Heaven's "Well done!" will be more
Give to God thy heart's devotion;
  Other service wins defeat.

3 Evening calls, the shadows lengthen;
  Art thou weak and shorn of pride?
God alone such hours can strengthen,
  Give thee light at eventide.
Morn and noon and eve,—Oh, hearken
  In the lingering of the light,
Ere the deeper shadows darken,
  And the coming of the night.
                    Emma Smuller Carter, 1894.

---

4 (GLORY). S. M.

1 Come, we that love the Lord,
    And let our joys be known;
  Join in a song of sweet accord,
    And thus surround the throne.

2 Let those refuse to sing
    Who never knew our God;
  But children of the heavenly King
    May speak their joys abroad.

3 The hill of Zion yields
    A thousand sacred sweets
  Before we reach the heavenly fields,.
    Or walk the golden streets.

4 Then let our songs abound,
    And every tear be dry;
  We're marching thro' Immanuel's ground
    To fairer worlds on high.
              Rev. Isaac Watts, 1709. Ab. and al. alt.

STILL WITH THEE.

5 SEYMOUR. 7.
CARL MARIA VON WEBER, 1826.
Arr. by HENRY WELLINGTON GREATOREX, 1849.

1. Soft-ly now the light of day Fades up-on my sight a-way;
Free from care, from la-bor free, Lord, I would commune with Thee.

2 Thou, whose all-pervading eye
Naught escapes without, within,
Pardon each infirmity,
Open fault, and secret sin.

3 Soon, for me, the light of day
Shall forever pass away:
Then, from sin and sorrow free,
Take me, Lord, to dwell with Thee.

4 Thou who, sinless, yet hast known
All of man's infirmity;
Then from Thine eternal throne,
Jesus, look with pitying eye.

Bp. George Washington Doane, 1824.

6 ARCADELT. S. M.
JACQUES ARCADELT, 1550.
Arr. by C. ARTHUR JACQUES, 1897.

1. Still, still with Thee, my God, I would de-sire to be:
By day, by night, at home, a-broad, I would be still with Thee.

Copyright, 1899, by Rev. James Carter.

2 With Thee, when dawn comes in,
And calls me back to care,
Each day returning to begin
With Thee, my God, in prayer.

3 With Thee amid the crowd
That throngs the busy mart,
To hear Thy voice, 'mid clamor loud,
Speak softly to my heart.

4 With Thee, when day is done,
And evening calms the mind;
The setting, as the rising, sun
With Thee my heart would find.

5 With Thee, in Thee, by faith
Abiding I would be;
By day, by night, in life, in death,
I would be still with Thee.

Rev. James Drummond Burns, 1856. Ab. and sl. alt.

EVENING PRAYER.

7 ANGELUS.
Softly, with expression.   Rev. RAYMOND DE WITT MALLARY, 1898.

Copyright, used by permission of Rev. J. E. Rankin, D. D.

1. Hark! it is the an-ge-lus, With soft ca-dence steal-ing,
Res-pite sweet it brings to us, And a ho-ly feel-ing.
Flood-ing now the sun-set air, Fad-ing and in-creas-ing,
Hands we fold for one brief pray'r From our la-bor ceas-ing.

2 Weary is earth's frequent lot,
   Crowded beyond bearing;
Ah, what comfort in the thought!
   God that lot is sharing.
Reassured, our toil we close,
   Speedier for delaying;
Sweeter, sweeter night's repose
   For this vesper praying.

3 And when sounds night's angelus,
   All our labors ended,
Be the setting sun to us
   As some vision splendid;
Then, hands folded as in prayer,
   Washed in blood, forgiven,
Wafted down to meet us there
   The sweet bells of heaven.
         Rev. Jeremiah Eames Rankin, 1898.

8 (ARCADELT). S. M.

1 The day, O Lord, is spent;
   Abide with us, and rest;
Our heart's desires are fully bent
   On making Thee our guest.

2 We have not reached that land,
   That happy land, as yet,
Where holy angels round Thee stand,
   Whose sun can never set.

3 Our sun is sinking now,
   Our day is almost o'er;
O Sun of Righteousness, do Thou
   Shine on us evermore!

4 The grace of Christ our Lord,
   The Father's boundless love,
The Spirit's blest communion, too,
   Be with us from above.
         Rev. John Mason Neale, 1842.

CLOSING DAY.

9 HALLE. 7. 6 l.   PETER RITTER, 1792.

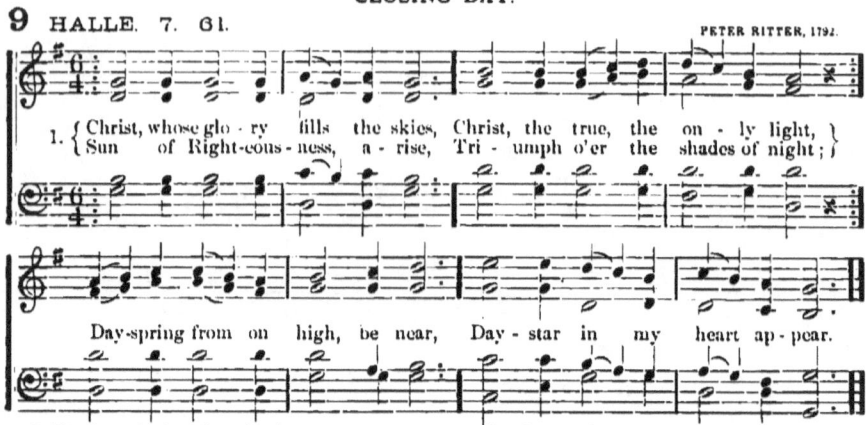

1. Christ, whose glory fills the skies, Christ, the true, the only light,
Sun of Righteousness, arise, Triumph o'er the shades of night;
Day-spring from on high, be near, Day-star in my heart appear.

2 Dark and cheerless is the morn,
  If Thy light is hid from me;
 Joyless is the day's return,
  Till Thy mercy's beams I see;
 Till thy inward light impart,
  Warmth and gladness to my heart.

3 Visit, then, this soul of mine;
  Pierce the gloom of sin and grief;
 Fill me, radiant Sun divine!
  Scatter all my unbelief;
 More and more Thyself display,
  Shining to the perfect day.
      Rev. Charles Wesley, 1740. Alt.

In the work of praise and prayer,
 Lord! I would converse with Thee:
Oh! behold me from above,
 Fill me with a Saviour's love.

2 Sin and sorrow, guilt and woe,
  Wither all my earthly joys;
 Naught can charm me here below,
  But my Saviour's melting voice:
 Lord! forgive—Thy grace restore,
  Make me Thine forevermore.

3 For the blessings of this day,
  For the mercies of this hour,
 For the gospel's cheering ray,
  For the Spirit's quickening power,—
 Grateful notes to Thee I raise;
  Oh! accept my song of praise.
      Thomas Hastings, 1831.

10

1 Now, from labor and from care,
  Evening shades have set me free;

11 MERRIAL. 6. 5.   JOSEPH BARNBY, 1868.

1. Now the day is over, Night is drawing nigh, Shadows of the evening Steal across the sky.
Shadows of the evening Steal across the sky.

2 Jesus, give the weary
   Calm and sweet repose;
  With Thy tenderest blessing
   May our eyelids close.

3 Grant to little children
   Visions bright of Thee;
  Guard the sailor tossing
   On the deep blue sea.

4 Through the long night-watches,
   May Thine angels spread
  Their white wings above me,
   Watching round my bed.

5 When the morning wakens,
   Then may I arise,
  Pure and fresh and sinless
   In Thy holy eyes.
      Rev. Sabine Baring-Gould, 1865. Ab.

EVENTIDE.

12 ANGELUS. L. M.   GEORG JOSEPHI, 1657.

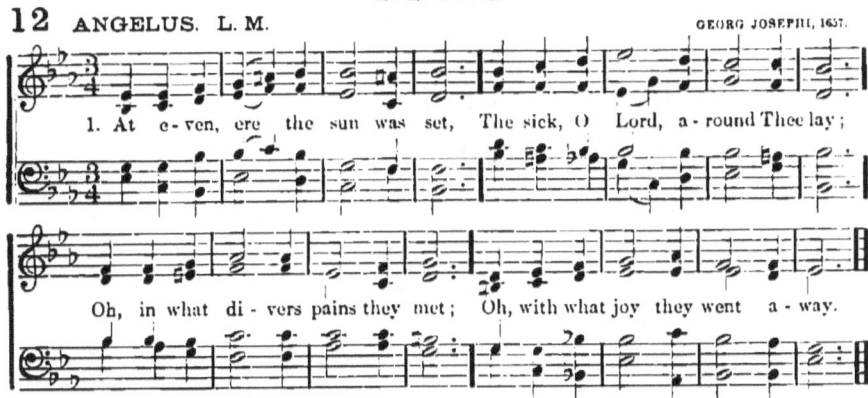

1. At e-ven, ere the sun was set, The sick, O Lord, a-round Thee lay;
Oh, in what di-vers pains they met; Oh, with what joy they went a-way.

2 Once more 'tis eventide, and we,
  Oppressed with various ills, draw near:
What if Thy form we cannot see?
  We know and feel that Thou art here.

3 O Saviour Christ, our woes dispel,
  For some are sick, and some are sad,
And some have never loved Thee well,
  And some have lost the love they had.

4 And some have found the world is vain,
  Yet from the world they break not free;
And some have friends who give them pain,
  Yet have not sought a friend in Thee.

5 And none, O Lord, has perfect rest,
  For none is wholly free from sin:
And they who fain would serve Thee best,
  Are conscious most of wrong within.

6 O Saviour Christ, Thou too art Man;
  Thou hast been troubled, tempted, tried;
Thy kind but searching glance can scan,
  The very wounds that shame would hide;

7 Thy touch has still its ancient power,
  No word from Thee can fruitless fall;
Hear in this solemn evening hour,
  And in Thy mercy heal us all.
          Rev. Henry Twells. 1868.

13

1 My God, how endless is Thy love!
  Thy gifts are every evening new;
And morning mercies from above,
  Gently distill like early dew.

2 Thou spread'st the curtains of the night,
  Great Guardian of my sleeping hours;
Thy sovereign word restores the light,
  And quickens all my drowsy powers.

3 I yield my powers to Thy command;
  To Thee I consecrate my days;
Perpetual blessings from Thine hand
  Demand perpetual songs of praise.
          Rev. Isaac Watts, 1709.

14

1 Thus far the Lord has led me on;
  Thus far His power prolongs my days;
And every evening shall make known
  Some fresh memorial of His grace.

2 Much of my time has run to waste,
  And I, perhaps, am near my home:
But He forgives my follies past,
  And gives me strength for days to come.

3 I lay my body down to sleep;
  Peace is the pillow for my head;
While well-appointed angels keep
  Their watchful stations round my bed.

4 Thus, when the night of death shall come,
  My flesh shall rest beneath the ground,
And wait Thy voice to break my tomb,
  With sweet salvation in the sound.
          Rev. Isaac Watts, 1709. Ab.

HEBRON. L. M.   LOWELL MASON, 1830.

EVENING.

15 VESPERALIS. 9.8. Rev. JAMES CARTER, 1894.

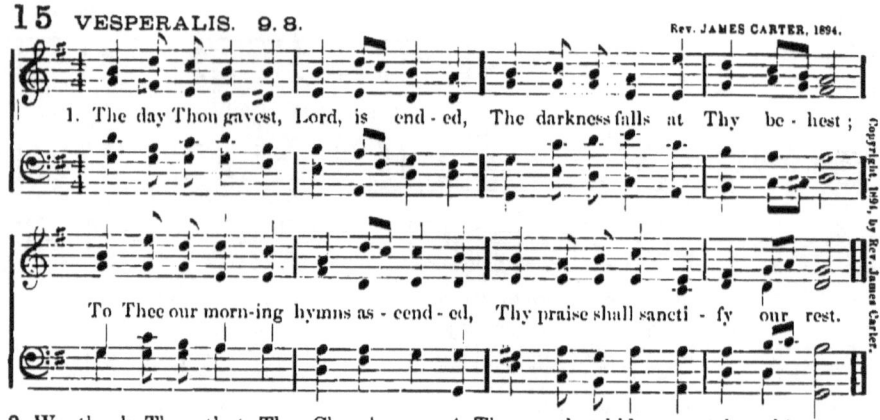

1. The day Thou gavest, Lord, is end-ed, The darkness falls at Thy be-hest; To Thee our morn-ing hymns as-cend-ed, Thy praise shall sancti-fy our rest.

2 We thank Thee that Thy Church un-
    sleeping,
  While earth rolls onward into light,
  Thro' all the world her watch is keeping,
    And rests not now by day or night.
3 As o'er each continent and island
    The dawn leads on another day,
  The voice of prayer is never silent,
    Nor dies the strain of praise away.

4 The sun that bids us rest is waking
    Our brethren 'neath the western sky,
  And hour by hour fresh lips are making
    Thy wondrous doings heard on high.
5 So be it, Lord; Thy Throne shall never,
    Like earth's proud empires, pass a-
      way;
  Thy Kingdom stands, and grows forever,
    Till all Thy creatures own Thy sway.
            Rev. John Ellerton, 1870.

16 HORA OCCIDUA. 6.5. Rev. JAMES CARTER, 1894.

1. Gen-tly falls the e-ven Of the Sab-bath day; Lord of earth and Heav-en Come to us, we pray.

2 Here in meek confession
    At Thy feet we bow;
  Pardon our transgression;
    Grant Thy blessing now.
3 Hush all evil passion;
    Guard the sin-enticed;
  Every spirit fashion
    Like our Master Christ.

4 When temptations sift us,
    Ere we yield or fall,
  May Thy grace uplift us;
    Bear us safe through all.
5 Till the dawn shall brighten
    And the shadows flee,
  May Thy love enlighten
    Those who rest in Thee.
            Rev. James Carter, 1894.

CLOSE OF SERVICE.

17. GOD BE WITH YOU.
WILLIAM G. TOMER, 1879.

2 God be with you till we meet again,
  'Neath His wings protecting hide you,
  Daily manna still divide you,
  God be with you till we meet again.

3 God be with you till we meet again,
  When life's perils thick confound you,
  Put His arms unfailing round you,
  God be with you till we meet again.

4 God be with you till we meet again,
  Keep love's banner floating o'er you,
  Smite death's threatening wave before you,
  God be with you till we meet again.

Rev. Jeremiah Eames Rankin, 1879.

IN THE GLOAMING.

18 EVENTIDE. 10. WILLIAM HENRY MONK, 1861.

1. A-bide with me: fast falls the e-ven-tide; The dark-ness deep-ens; Lord, with me a-bide; When oth-er help-ers fail, and com-forts flee, Help of the help-less, oh, a-bide with me.

2 Swift to its close ebbs out life's little day;
  Earth's joys grow dim, its glories pass away;
  Change and decay in all around I see;
  O Thou, who changest not, abide with me.

3 I need Thy presence every passing hour:
  What but Thy grace can foil the tempter's power?
  Who like Thyself my guide and stay can be?
  Through cloud and sunshine, oh, abide with me.

4 I fear no foe, with Thee at hand to bless;
  Ills have no weight, and tears no bitterness;
  Where is death's sting? where, grave, thy victory?
  I triumph still, if Thou abide with me.
            Rev. Henry Francis Lyte, 1847. Ab.

HURSLEY. L. M. PETER RITTER, 1792.
Arr. by WILLIAM HENRY MONK, 1861.

1. Sun of my soul, Thou Sav-iour dear, It is not night if Thou be near: Oh, may no earth-born cloud a-rise To hide Thee from Thy ser-vant's eyes.

DEPARTING DAY.

19 ROBINSON. 6. 4. 6. 4. 6. 6. 6. 4. Rev. JAMES CARTER, 1896.

1. Softly the twilight fades Into the west, Softly the evening shades Call man to rest. Thou, whose unclouded sight Pierces the gloom of night, Pour on us heav'nly light, And make us blest.

2 Far o'er the stars that shine
   Deep in our sky,
Worships that host of Thine,
   Holy on high.
Lowly on earth are we
Who lift our prayer to Thee.
Hear Thou our humble plea:
   Saviour be nigh.

3 Spirit, whose brooding love,
   While nature sleeps,
Hovers in might above
   The viewless deeps,
Unto Thy children bend,
Strength to our weakness lend,
Make us with joy ascend
   Thy heavenly steeps.

4 Lord God, our dwelling-place
   Age after age,
Protect us by Thy grace
   From Satan's rage;
Bring us to that fair shore
Where Christ is gone before.
Thou shalt be evermore
   Our heritage.

                              Rev James Carter, 1896.

---

20 (HURSLEY). L. M.

1 Sun of my soul! Thou Saviour dear,
It is not night if Thou be near:
Oh, may no earth-born cloud arise
To hide Thee from Thy servant's eyes!

2 When the soft dews of kindly sleep
My wearied eyelids gently steep,
Be my last thought, how sweet to rest
Forever on the Saviour's breast.

3 Abide with me from morn till eve,
For without Thee I cannot live;
Abide with me when night is nigh,
For without Thee I dare not die.

4 If some poor wandering child of Thine
Have spurned, to-day, the voice divine;
Now, Lord, the gracious work begin;
Let him no more lie down in sin.

5 Watch by the sick; enrich the poor
With blessings from Thy boundless store;
Be every mourner's sleep to-night,
Like infant's slumbers, pure and light.

6 Come near and bless us when we wake,
Ere through the world our way we take;
Till, in the ocean of Thy love,
We lose ourselves in Heaven above.
                       Rev. John Keble, 1827. Ab.

LIGHT AT EVENTIME.

21 IGNATIUS. S. M. HENRY JOHN GAUNTLETT, 1843.

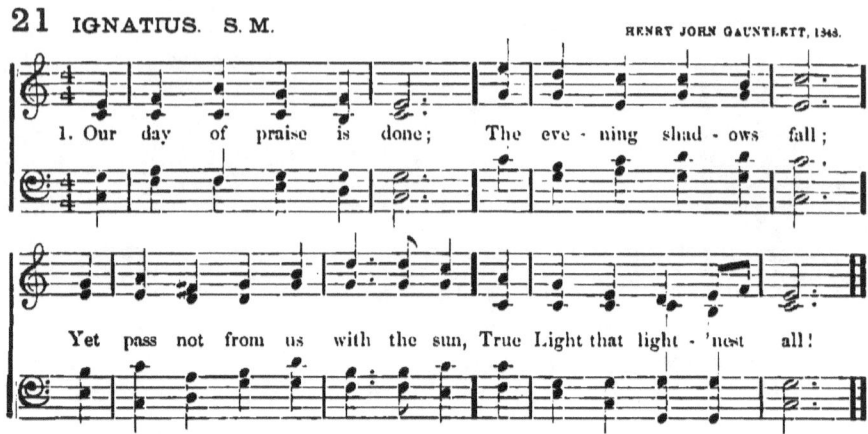

1. Our day of praise is done; The evening shadows fall; Yet pass not from us with the sun, True Light that lightenest all!

2 Around Thy throne on high,
   Where night can never be,
The white-robed harpers of the sky
   Bring ceaseless hymns to Thee.

3 Too faint our anthems here;
   Too soon of praise we tire;
But oh, the strains how full and clear
   Of that eternal choir!

4 Yet, Lord, to Thy dear will
   If Thou attune the heart,
We in Thine angels' music still
   May bear our lower part.

5 Shine Thou within us, then,
   A day that knows no end,
Till songs of angels and of men
   In perfect praise shall blend.

Rev. John Ellerton, 1867, 1871. Ab.

22 CONRAD. 8. 8. 8. 4. Rev. JAMES CARTER, 1898.

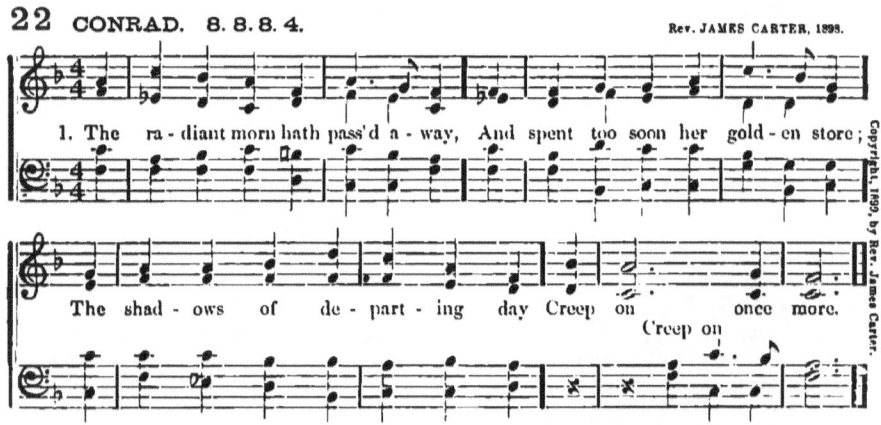

1. The radiant morn hath pass'd away, And spent too soon her golden store; The shadows of departing day Creep on once more.

Copyright, 1899, by Rev. James Carter.

2 Our life is but a fading dawn;
   Its glorious noon how quickly past!
Lend us, O Christ, when all is gone,
   Safe home at last.

3 Oh, by Thy soul-inspiring grace,
   Uplift our hearts to realms on high;
Help us to look to that bright place
   Beyond the sky;—

4 Where light and life and joy and peace
   In undivided empire reign,
And thronging angels never cease
   Their deathless strain;—

5 Where saints are clothed in spotless white,
   And evening shadows never fall;
Where Thou, eternal Light of light,
   Art Lord of all!

Rev. Godfrey Thring, 1864.

THE MERCY SEAT.

23 RETREAT. L. M. THOMAS HASTINGS, 1840.

1. From ev-'ry stormy wind that blows, From ev-'ry swelling tide of woes, There is a calm, a sure re-treat; 'Tis found be-neath the mer-cy-seat.

2 There is a place where Jesus sheds
The oil of gladness on our heads,—
A place, than all besides, more sweet;
It is the blood-bought mercy-seat.

3 There is a scene where spirits blend,
Where friend holds fellowship with friend;
Though sundered far, by faith they meet
Around one common mercy-seat.

4 There, there, on eagle wings we soar,
And time and sense seem all no more,
And Heaven comes down our souls to greet,
And glory crowns the mercy-seat!

5 Oh! let my hand forget her skill,
My tongue be silent, cold, and still,
This throbbing heart forget to beat,
If I forget the mercy-seat.
　　　　Rev. Hugh Stowell. 1831. Ab.

24 HORTON. 7. XAVIER SCHNYDER VON WARTENSEE, 1826.

1. Come, my soul, thy suit pre-pare, Je-sus loves to an-swer pray'r; He Him-self has bid thee pray, Therefore will not say thee nay.

2 With my burden I begin:
Lord, remove this load of sin;
Let Thy blood, for sinners spilt,
Set my conscience free from guilt.

3 Lord, I come to Thee for rest,
Take possession of my breast;
There, Thy sovereign right maintain,
And, without a rival, reign.

4 While I am a pilgrim here,
Let Thy love my spirit cheer;
As my Guide, my Guard, my Friend,
Lead me to my journey's end.

5 Show me what I have to do,
Every hour my strength renew;
Let me live a life of faith,
Let me die Thy people's death.
　　　　Rev. John Newton, 1779. Ab.

THE HOUR OF PRAYER.

25 ELLERTON. 10. EDWARD JOHN HOPKINS, 1866.

1. Saviour, again to Thy dear Name we raise
With one accord our parting hymn of praise;
We rise to bless Thee ere our worship cease,
And now, departing, wait Thy word of peace.

2 Grant us Thy peace upon our homeward way;
With Thee began, with Thee shall end the day;
Guard Thou the lips from sin, the hearts from shame,
That in this house have called upon Thy name.

3 Grant us Thy peace, Lord, through the coming night;
Turn Thou for us its darkness into light;
From harm and danger keep Thy children free,
For dark and light are both alike to Thee.

4 Grant us Thy peace throughout our earthly life,
Our balm in sorrow, and our stay in strife;
Then, when Thy voice shall bid our conflict cease,
Call us, O Lord, to Thine eternal peace.

Rev. John Ellerton, 1866, 1868. V. 1 alt.

---

26 (ALMSGIVING). 8.8.8.4.

1 My God, is any hour so sweet,
　From blush of morn to evening star,
As that which calls me to Thy feet,
　The hour of prayer?

2 Blest is that tranquil hour of morn,
　And blest that solemn hour of eve,
When, on the wings of prayer upborne,
　The world I leave.

3 Then is my strength by Thee renewed;
　Then are my sins by Thee forgiven;
Then dost Thou cheer my solitude
　With hopes of Heaven.

4 No words can tell what sweet relief
　Here for my every want I find;
What strength for warfare, balm for grief,
　What peace of mind.

5 Hushed is each doubt, gone every fear;
　My spirit seems in Heaven to stay;
And e'en the penitential tear
　Is wiped away.

6 Lord, till I reach that blissful shore,
　No privilege so dear shall be
As thus my inmost soul to pour
　In prayer to Thee.

Miss Charlotte Elliott, 1829, 1836. Ab.

THE UNFAILING FRIEND.

27 ERIE. 8. 7. D.   CHARLES CROZAT CONVERSE, 1868.

2 Have we trials and temptations?
    Is there trouble anywhere?
   We should never be discouraged—
    Take it to the Lord in prayer.
   Can we find a friend so faithful,
    Who will all our sorrows share?
   Jesus knows our every weakness:
    Take it to the Lord in prayer.

3 Are we weak and heavy laden,
    Cumbered with a load of care?
   Precious Saviour, still our refuge!
    Take it to the Lord in prayer.
   Do thy friends despise, forsake thee?
    Take it to the Lord in prayer;
   In His arms He'll take and shield thee;
    Thou wilt find a solace there.
                    Joseph Scriven, 1855.

ALMSGIVING. 8. 8. 8. 4.   Rev. JOHN BACCHUS DYKES, 1875.

THE MIGHT OF PRAYER.

28 BARNEGAT. 12. 11. Rev. JAMES CARTER, 1895.

1. Oh, pray ye for others: the show-ers of Heav-en
Hang heav-y, a-wait-ing the voice of your prayer,
That bread to the fam-ish-ing free-ly be giv-en,
And strength un-to weak-ness and hope to de-spair.
Refrain. Lento. Oh, pray ye for oth-ers, for bless-ing now pray.

2 Oh, pray ye for others: temptation and trial
    Will strike at the faith of the soldier of Christ;
    The ambush of Satan cause startled denial,
    And shipwreck may come to the soul sin-enticed.

3 Oh, ne'er can ye measure the might of petition,
    To rescue the helpless and succor the tried,
    To melt the defiant to fitting contrition,
    To win the lost souls to the Saviour who died.

4 Oh, pray ye for others, that Christ's love may glisten
    In eyes that are pleading for truth and for God;
    Oh, pray ye for others, that dull ears may listen,
    And feet that are wandering, turn back to the road.

5 Oh, pray ye for others, the hearts that are lonely,
    The lives that are tempted by pleasure or fame,
    That every disciple may love Jesus only,
    May live to His glory and honor His Name.
                                Rev. James Carter, 1895.

THE WORD OF GOD.

29　UXBRIDGE. L. M.　　　　　　　　　　　　LOWELL MASON, 1830.

1. God, in the gospel of His Son, Makes His eternal counsels known, Where love in all its glory shines, And truth is drawn in fairest lines.

2　Here sinners of an humble frame,
　　May taste His grace and learn His name;
　　May read, in characters of blood,
　　The wisdom, power, and grace of God.

3　The prisoner here may break his chains;
　　The weary rest from all his pains;
　　The captive feel his bondage cease;
　　The mourner find the way of peace.

4　Here faith reveals to mortal eyes
　　A brighter world beyond the skies;
　　Here shines the light which guides our way
　　From earth to realms of endless day.

5　Oh, grant us grace, Almighty Lord,
　　To read and mark Thy holy word;
　　Its truth with meekness to receive,
　　And by its holy precepts live.
　　　　Rev. Benjamin Beddome, 1787. Ab. and alt.
　　　　Rev. Thomas Cotterill, 1819.

30　CHESTERFIELD. C. M.　　　　　　　　　　Rev. THOMAS HAWEIS, 1792.

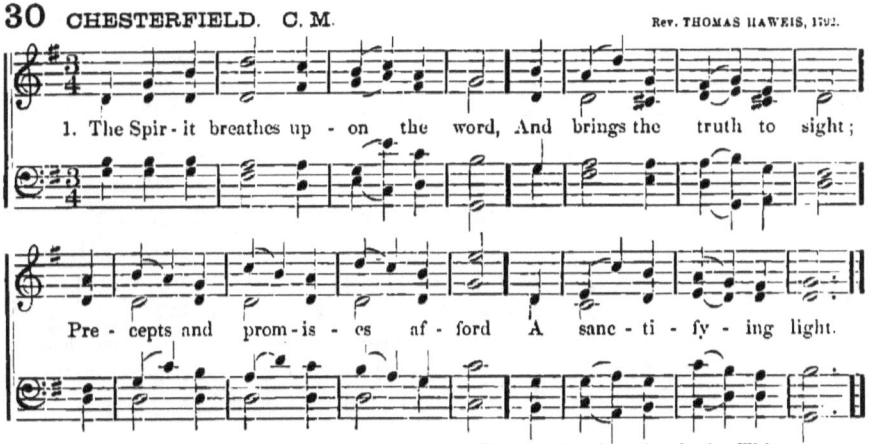

1. The Spirit breathes upon the word, And brings the truth to sight; Precepts and promises afford A sanctifying light.

2　A glory gilds the sacred page,
　　　Majestic, like the sun;
　　It gives a light to every age;—
　　　It gives, but borrows none.

3　The Hand, that gave it, still supplies
　　　The gracious light and heat;
　　Its truths upon the nations rise.—
　　　They rise, but never set.

4　Let everlasting thanks be Thine,
　　　For such a bright display,
　　As makes a world of darkness shine
　　　With beams of heavenly day.

5　My soul rejoices to pursue
　　　The steps of Him I love,
　　Till glory breaks upon my view,
　　　In brighter worlds above.
　　　　　　　William Cowper, 1779. Ab.

GOD.

31 LOUVAN. L. M.
VIRGIL CORYDON TAYLOR, 1847.

1. Lord of all being; throned afar, Thy glory flames from sun and star;
Center and soul of ev-'ry sphere, Yet to each loving heart how near!

2 Sun of our life, Thy quickening ray
Sheds on our path the glow of day;
Star of our hope, Thy softened light
Cheers the long watches of the night.

3 Our midnight is Thy smile withdrawn;
Our noontide is Thy gracious dawn;
Our rainbow arch Thy mercy's sign;
All, save the clouds of sin, are Thine!

4 Lord of all life, below, above,
Whose light is truth, whose warmth is love,
Before Thy ever-blazing throne
We ask no luster of our own.

5 Grant us Thy truth to make us free,
And kindling hearts that burn for Thee,
Till all Thy living altars claim
One holy light, one heavenly flame!

Oliver Wendell Holmes, 1848.

32 DUNDEE. C. M.
CHRISTOPHER TYE, 1553.

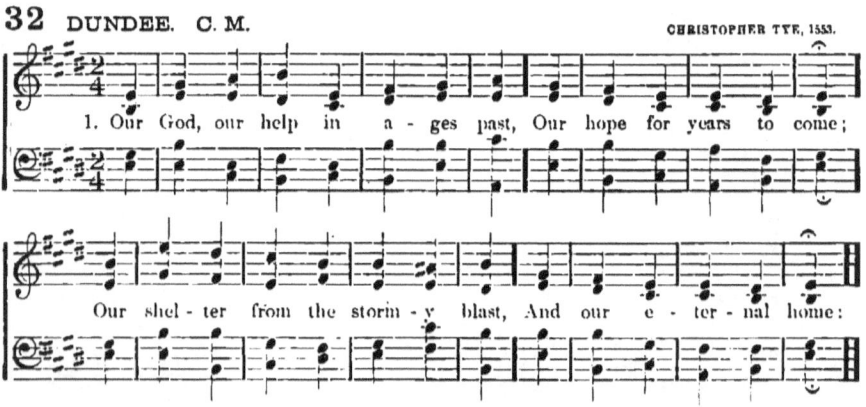

1. Our God, our help in ages past, Our hope for years to come;
Our shelter from the storm-y blast, And our eternal home:

2 Before the hills in order stood,
Or earth received her frame,
From everlasting Thou art God,
To endless years the same.

3 A thousand ages, in Thy sight,
Are like an evening gone;
Short as the watch that ends the night,
Before the rising sun.

4 Time, like an ever-rolling stream,
Bears all its sons away;
They fly, forgotten, as a dream
Dies at the opening day.

5 Our God, our help in ages past,
Our hope for years to come,
Be Thou our guard while troubles last,
And our eternal home.

Rev. Isaac Watts, 1719. Ab.

GOD IS LOVE.

33 MANOAH. C. M.
GIOACCHINO ANTONIO ROSSINI.
Arr. by HENRY WELLINGTON GREATOREX, 1851.

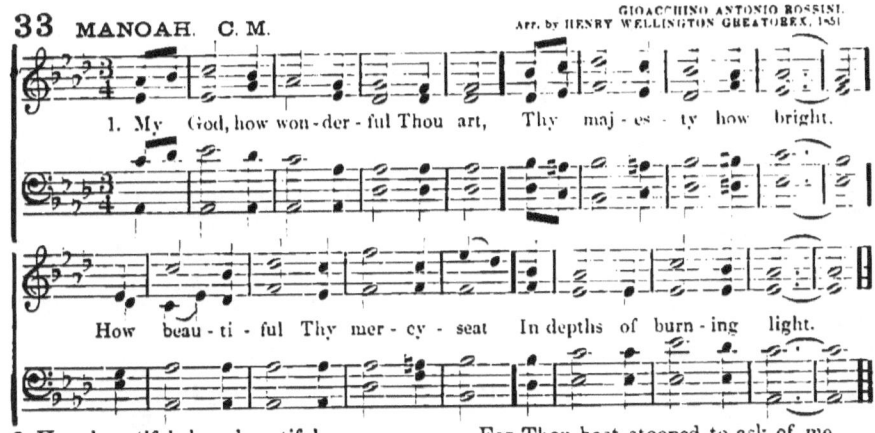

1. My God, how won-der-ful Thou art, Thy maj-es-ty how bright,
How beau-ti-ful Thy mer-cy-seat In depths of burn-ing light.

2 How beautiful, how beautiful
   The sight of Thee must be,
Thine endless wisdom, boundless power,
   And awful purity.

3 Oh, how I fear Thee, living God,
   With deepest, tenderest fears,
And worship Thee with trembling hope;
   And penitential tears.

4 Yet I may love Thee too, O Lord,
   Almighty as Thou art;

5 For Thou hast stooped to ask of me
   The love of my poor heart.

5 No earthly Father loves like Thee,
   No mother half so mild,
Bears and forbears, as Thou hast done,
   With me, Thy sinful child.

6 Father of Jesus, love's reward,
   What rapture will it be,
Prostrate before Thy throne to lie,
   And gaze, and gaze on Thee.
       Rev. Frederick William Faber, 1848. Ab.

34 CARTER. 8. 7.
Rev. EDMUND SARDINSON CARTER, 1874.

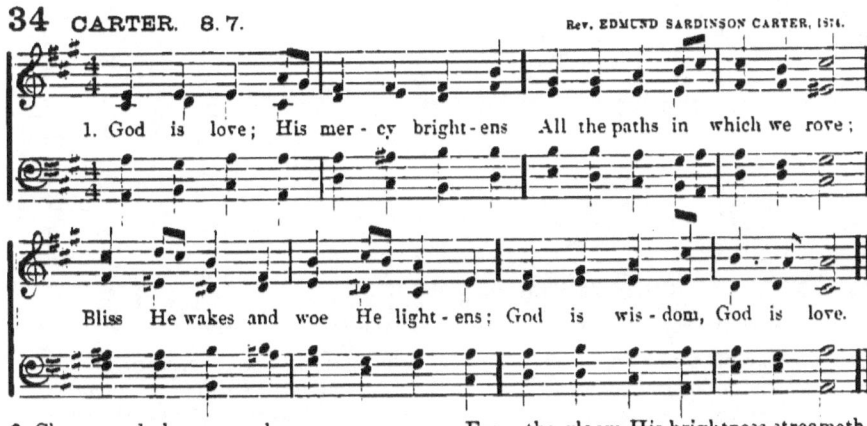

1. God is love; His mer-cy bright-ens All the paths in which we rove;
Bliss He wakes and woe He light-ens; God is wis-dom, God is love.

2 Chance and change are busy ever;
   Man decays, and ages move;
But His mercy waneth never;
   God is wisdom, God is love.

3 Ev'n the hour that darkest seemeth,
   Will His changeless goodness prove;

From the gloom His brightness streameth,
   God is wisdom, God is love.

4 He with earthly cares entwineth
   Hope and comfort from above;
Everywhere His glory shineth;
   God is wisdom, God is love.
       Sir John Bowring, 1825. Ab.

THE PRAISE OF GOD.

35 NETTLETON. 8. 7. D.
Rev. JOHN WYETH, 1812.

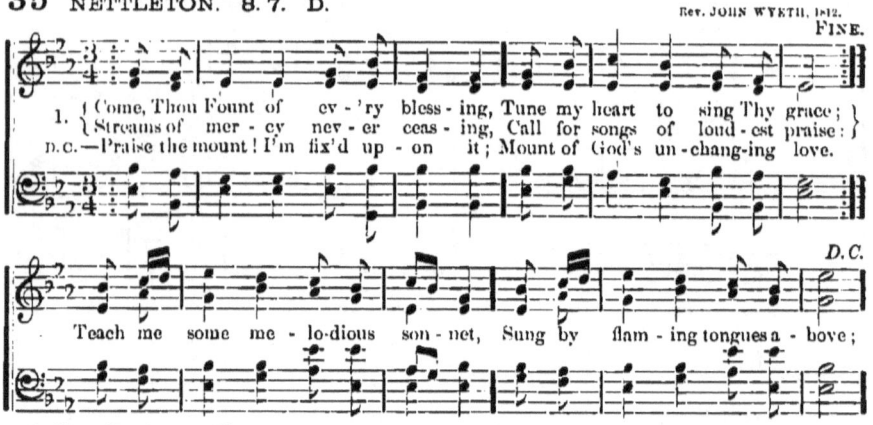

1. Come, Thou Fount of ev-'ry bless-ing, Tune my heart to sing Thy grace;
Streams of mer-cy nev-er ceas-ing, Call for songs of loud-est praise:
D.C.—Praise the mount! I'm fix'd up-on it; Mount of God's un-chang-ing love.

Teach me some me-lo-dious son-net, Sung by flam-ing tongues a-bove;

2 Here I raise my Ebenezer,
　Hither by Thy help I'm come;
And I hope, by Thy good pleasure,
　Safely to arrive at home;
Jesus sought me, when a stranger,
　Wandering from the fold of God;
He, to rescue me from danger,
　Interposed His precious blood.

3 Oh, to grace how great a debtor,
　Daily I'm constrained to be;
Let that grace now, like a fetter,
　Bind my wandering heart to Thee:
Prone to wander, Lord, I feel it,
　Prone to leave the God I love;
Here's my heart, oh, take and seal it,
　Seal it from Thy courts above.
　　　　Rev. Robert Robinson, 1757.

36 LAUD. C. M.
Rev. JOHN BACCHUS DYKES, 1862.

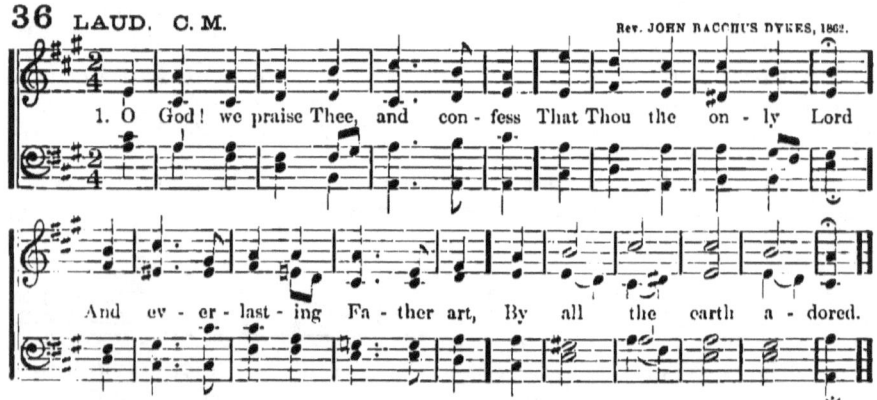

1. O God! we praise Thee, and con-fess That Thou the on-ly Lord
And ev-er-last-ing Fa-ther art, By all the earth a-dored.

2 To Thee all angels cry aloud;
　To Thee the powers on high,
Both cherubim and seraphim,
　Continually do cry:—
3 O Holy, Holy, Holy Lord,
　Whom heavenly hosts obey,
The world is with the glory filled
　Of Thy majestic sway!

4 The apostles' glorious company,
　And prophets crowned with light,
With all the martyrs' noble host,
　Thy constant praise recite.
5 The holy Church throughout the world,
　O Lord, confesses Thee,
That Thou the eternal Father art,
　Of boundless majesty.
　　　Unknown Author, 5th. Century.
　　　Tr. by Bp. John Patrick, 1679.
　　　Alt. by Tate and Brady, 1700.

THE EVERLASTING GOD.

37 AURELIA. 7. 6. D.   SAMUEL SEBASTIAN WESLEY, c. 1868.

1. O God, the Rock of A - ges, Who ev - er-more hast been, What time the tempest rag - es, Our dwell-ing-place se - rene: Be - fore Thy first cre - a - tions, O Lord, the same as now, To end-less gen - er - a - tions, The Ev - er - last-ing Thou!

2 Our years are like the shadows
   On sunny hills that lie,
Or grasses in the meadows
   That blossom but to die:
A sleep, a dream, a story,
   By strangers quickly told,
An unremaining glory
   Of things that soon are old.

3 O Thou who canst not slumber,
   Whose light grows never pale,
Teach us aright to number
   Our years before they fail.
On us Thy mercy lighten,
   On us Thy goodness rest,
And let Thy Spirit brighten
   The hearts Thyself hast blessed.

4 Lord, crown our faith's endeavor
   With beauty and with grace,
Till, clothed in light forever,
   We see Thee face to face:
A joy no language measures,
   A fountain brimming o'er,
An endless flow of pleasures,
   An ocean without shore.
      Bp. Edward Henry Bickersteth, 1862.

38

1 O One with God the Father
   In majesty and might,
The brightness of His glory,
   Eternal Light of light;
O'er this our home of darkness
   Thy rays are streaming now;
The shadows flee before Thee,
   The world's true light art Thou.

2 Yet, Lord, we see but darkly:—
   O Heavenly Light, arise,
Dispel these mists that shroud us,
   And hide Thee from our eyes.
We long to track the footprints
   That Thou Thyself hast trod;
We long to see the pathway
   That leads to Thee our God.

3 O Jesus, shine around us
   With radiance of Thy grace;
O Jesus, turn upon us
   The brightness of Thy face.
We need no star to guide us,
   As on our way we press,
If Thou Thy light vouchsafest,
   O Sun of righteousness.
      Bp. William Walsham How, 1871.

THE PRAISE OF GOD.

39 OLD HUNDRED. L. M. LOUIS BOURGEOIS, 1551.

1. Be-fore Je-ho-vah's aw-ful throne, Ye na-tions bow with sa-cred joy:
Know that the Lord is God a-lone: He can cre-ate, and He de-stroy.

2 His sovereign power, without our aid,
   Made us of clay, and formed us men;
   And when, like wandering sheep, we stray'd,
   He brought us to His fold again.

3 We are His people, we His care,—
   Our souls, and all our mortal frame:
   What lasting honors shall we rear,
   Almighty Maker! to Thy name?

4 We'll crowd Thy gates with thankful songs,
   High as the heavens our voices raise;
   And earth, with her ten thousand tongues,
   Shall fill Thy courts with sounding praise.

5 Wide as the world is Thy command,
   Vast as eternity, Thy love;
   Firm as a rock Thy truth shall stand,
   When rolling years shall cease to move.

Rev. Isaac Watts, 1719. Ab.
Alt. by Rev. John Wesley, 1736.

CORONATION. C. M. OLIVER HOLDEN, 1793.

1. All hail the pow'r of Je-sus' Name! Let an-gels pros-trate fall;
Bring forth the roy-al di-a-dem, And crown Him Lord of all,
Bring forth the roy-al di-a-dem, And crown Him Lord of all.

LORD OF ALL.

40 LYONS. 10. 11.   FRANCIS JOSEPH HAYDN, 1770

1. Oh, worship the King, all-glorious above, And gratefully sing His power and His love; Our Shield and Defender, the Ancient of days, Pavilion'd in splendor, and girded with praise.

2 Oh, tell of His might, and sing of His grace,
Whose robe is the light, whose canopy space;
His chariots of wrath the deep thunder-clouds form,
And dark is His path on the wings of the storm.

3 Thy bountiful care what tongue can recite?
It breathes in the air, it shines in the light,
It streams from the hills, it descends to the plain,
And sweetly distills in the dew and the rain.

4 Frail children of dust, and feeble as frail,
In Thee do we trust, nor find Thee to fail;
Thy mercies how tender! how firm to the end!
Our Maker, Defender, Redeemer, and Friend.

Sir Robert Grant, 1833. Ab.

---

41 (CORONATION). C. M.

1 All hail the power of Jesus' Name!
   Let angels prostrate fall;
Bring forth the royal diadem,
   And crown Him Lord of all.

2 Crown Him, ye martyrs of our God,
   Who from His altar call;
Extol the stem of Jesse's rod,
   And crown Him Lord of all.

3 Ye chosen seed of Israel's race,
   Ye ransomed from the fall;
Hail Him, who saves you by His grace,
   And crown Him Lord of all.

4 Sinners, whose love can ne'er forget
   The wormwood and the gall;
Go, spread your trophies at His feet,
   And crown Him Lord of all.

5 Let every kindred, every tribe,
   On this terrestrial ball,
To Him all majesty ascribe,
   And crown Him Lord of all.

6 Oh, that with yonder sacred throng,
   We at His feet may fall;
We'll join the everlasting song,
   And crown Him Lord of all.

Rev. Edward Perronet, 1779, 1780. Ab.
Rev. John Rippon, 1787.

THE ANGELS' SONG.

42 CAROL. C. M. D. RICHARD STORRS WILLIS, 1850.

1. It came upon the midnight clear, That glorious song of old, From angels bending near the earth, To touch their harps of gold;
D.S.—earth in solemn stillness lay, To hear the angels sing.
"Peace to the earth, good-will to men, From Heav'n's all gracious King:" The

2 Still through the cloven skies they come,
  With peaceful wings unfurled;
And still celestial music floats
  O'er all the weary world;
Above its sad and lowly plains
  They bend on heavenly wing,
And ever o'er its Babel sounds,
  The blessed angels sing.

3 O ye, beneath life's crushing load,
  Whose forms are bending low,
Who toil along the climbing way,
  With painful steps and slow;—
Look up! for glad and golden hours
  Come swiftly on the wing;
Oh, rest beside the weary road,
  And hear the angels sing!

4 For lo! the days are hastening on,
  By prophet-bards foretold,
When with the ever-circling years
  Comes round the age of gold!
When peace shall over all the earth
  Its final splendors fling,
And the whole world send back the song
  Which now the angels sing!
    Rev. Edmund Hamilton Sears, 1850. Ab. and sl. alt.

43 (or CHRISTMAS).

1 While shepherds watched their flocks by
    All seated on the ground;   [night,
  The angel of the Lord came down,
    And glory shone around.
  "Fear not," said he,—for mighty dread
    Had seized their troubled mind,—
  "Glad tidings of great joy I bring,
    To you and all mankind.

2 "To you, in David's town this day,
    Is born of David's line,
  The Saviour, who is Christ, the Lord,
    And this shall be the sign:—
  The heavenly Babe you there shall find
    To human view displayed,
  All meanly wrapped in swathing bands,
    And in a manger laid."

3 Thus spake the seraph, and forthwith
    Appeared a shining throng
  Of angels, praising God, who thus
    Addressed their joyful song:—
  "All glory be to God on high,
    And to the earth be peace;
  Good-will henceforth from Heaven to men
    Begin, and never cease!"
    Nahum Tate, 1702.

AT THE MANGER.

44 BETHLEHEM. 8.7.8.7.7.7.   Rev. JAMES CARTER, 1880.

1. Night of won-der, night of glo-ry, Such as time has nev-er seen! Theme of old pro-phet-ic sto-ry, Night all sol-emn and se-rene: Sweet-est si-lence, soft-est blue That earth's dark-ness ev-er knew!

2 Happy city, dearest, fairest,
   Lonely, tranquil Bethlehem !
Least and lowliest, richest, rarest,
   David's city, Judah's gem ;
Out of thee there comes the light
That dispelleth all our night.

3 In thee Heaven and earth are meeting ;
   Lo ! there comes the angel-throng :
We give back the heavenly greeting,
   Joining in the holy song,—
Song of festival and mirth,
Song of morning to the earth.

4 Now to thee thy King descendeth,
   Laid upon a woman's knee ;
To thy gates His steps He bendeth,
   To the manger cometh He ;
David's Lord and David's Son,
This His cradle and His throne.

5 Light of life, Thou liest yonder,
   Mystery of mighty love ;
Naught from Thee our souls shall sunder
   Naught from us shall Thee remove.
Take these hearts, and let them be
Throne and cradle both for Thee.
                      Rev. Horatius Bonar, 1878.

CHRISTMAS. C. M.   GEORGE FREDERICK HANDEL, 1728.

THE STORY OF LOVE.

45 KENOSIS.
Rev. JAMES CARTER, 1897.

1. Sing of His love, who descended,
Coming in meekness to earth;
Godhead and manhood are blended,
Holy and marvelous birth.
He to His own as a stranger
Came to the inn's lowly door;
Naught but the clover-strewn manger
Welcomed the Child of the poor.

REF.—Sing we the Lord who has bought us,
Jesus who came from above,
Learning the lesson He taught us,
Great is the story of love.

2 Think of His fast on the mountain,
 Where on the serpent He trod;
Weary by Gerezim's fountain,
 Won He the sinner to God.
Yea, though the throngs heard Him gladly,
 Healed and enlightened and fed;
Lonely He wandered and sadly,
 Owning no rest for His head.

3 Think of the hate that betrayed Him,
 Think of the cross of His pain;
Come, see the place where they laid Him.
 Lo! He is risen again,
Love and compassion so tender
 Unto the end may we see!
Lord of our life, we must render
 Love and devotion to Thee.

Rev. James Carter, 1897.

46 (ANTIOCH). C. M.

1 Joy to the world, the Lord is come!
 Let earth receive her King;
Let every heart prepare Him room,
 And Heaven and nature sing.

2 Joy to the world, the Saviour reigns;
 Let men their songs employ;
While fields and floods, rocks, hills, and
 Repeat the sounding joy. [plains

3 No more let sin and sorrow grow,
 Nor thorns infest the ground;
He comes to make His blessings flow
 Far as the curse is found.

4 He rules the world with truth and grace,
 And makes the nations prove
The glories of His righteousness,
 And wonders of His love.

Rev. Isaac Watts, 1719.

THE COMING OF THE KING.

47 DIX. 7. 6 l.

CONRAD KOCHER, 1838.
WILLIAM HENRY MONK, 1861.

1. As with gladness men of old Did the guiding star behold,
   As with joy they hailed its light, Leading onward, beaming bright;
   So, most gracious Lord, may we Evermore be led to Thee.

2 As with joyful steps they sped,
  Saviour, to Thy manger bed,
  There to bend the knee before
  Thee whom Heaven and earth adore;
  So may we with willing feet
  Ever seek the mercy-seat.

3 As they offered gifts most rare
  At Thy cradle rude and bare,
  So may we with holy joy,
  Pure and free from sin's alloy,
  All our costliest treasures bring,
  Christ, to Thee our heavenly King.

4 Holy Jesus, every day
  Keep us in the narrow way;
  And, when earthly things are past,
  Bring our ransomed souls at last
  Where they need no star to guide,
  Where no clouds Thy glory hide.

William Chatterton Dix, 1860.

ANTIOCH. C. M.

GEORGE FREDERICK HANDEL, 1741.
Arr. by LOWELL MASON, 1836.

1. Joy to the world, the Lord is come? Let earth receive her King; Let ev-'ry heart prepare Him room, And Heav'n and nature sing, And Heav'n and nature sing, And Heav'n, And Heav'n and nature sing, And Heav'n and nature sing.

ONE ABOVE ALL OTHERS.

48 CALVARY. C.M.

LUDWIG SPOHR, 1835.
Arr. by C. ARTHUR JACQUES, 1895.

1. We may not climb the heav'n-ly steeps To bring the Lord Christ down;
In vain we search the low-est deeps, For Him no depths can drown.

2 But warm, sweet, tender, even yet
  A present help is He;
  And faith has yet its Olivet,
  And love its Galilee.

3 The healing of the seamless dress
  Is by our beds of pain;
  We touch Him in life's throng and press,
  And we are whole again.

4 Thro' Him the first fond prayers are said
  Our lips of childhood frame;
  The last low whispers of our dead
  Are burdened with His Name.

5 O Lord and Master of us all,
  Whate'er our name or sign,
  We own Thy sway, we hear Thy call,
  We test our lives by Thine!
  John Greenleaf Whittier, 1856. Ab.

49

1 Thou art the Way: to Thee alone
  From sin and death we flee;
  And he who would the Father seek,
  Must seek Him, Lord, by Thee.

2 Thou art the Truth: Thy word alone
  True wisdom can impart;
  Thou only canst instruct the mind,
  And purify the heart.

3 Thou art the Life: the rending tomb
  Proclaims Thy conquering arm;
  And those who put their trust in Thee
  Nor death nor hell shall harm.

4 Thou art the Way, the Truth, the Life:
  Grant us to know that Way;
  That Truth to keep, that Life to win,
  Which leads to endless day.
  Bp. George Washington Doane, 1824.

50

1 Lord, as to Thy dear cross we flee,
  And plead to be forgiven,
  So let Thy life our pattern be,
  And form our souls for Heaven.

2 Help us, through good report and ill,
  Our daily cross to bear;
  Like Thee, to do our Father's will,
  Our brethren's griefs to share.

3 If joy shall at Thy bidding fly,
  And grief's dark day come on,
  We in our turn would meekly cry,
  Father, Thy will be done.

4 Kept peaceful in the midst of strife,
  Forgiving and forgiven,
  Oh, may we lead the pilgrim's life,
  And follow Thee to Heaven.
  Rev. John Hampden Gurney, 1838. Ab.

AVON. C. M.

HUGH WILSON, 1825.

51 ROCKINGHAM. L. M.
LOWELL MASON, 1832.

1. My dear Redeemer, and my Lord, I read my duty in Thy word; But in Thy life the law appears, Drawn out in living characters.

2 Such was Thy truth, and such Thy zeal,
Such deference to Thy Father's will,
Such love, and meekness so divine,
I would transcribe and make them mine.

3 Cold mountains and the midnight air
Witnessed the fervor of Thy prayer;
The desert Thy temptations knew,
Thy conflict and Thy victory too.

4 Be Thou my pattern; make me bear
More of Thy gracious image here;
Then God, the Judge, shall own my name
Among the followers of the Lamb.

Rev. Isaac Watts, 1709.

52 GERMANY. L. M.
Subject from LUDWIG von BEETHOVEN.
WILLIAM GARDINER'S Sacred Melodies, 1815.

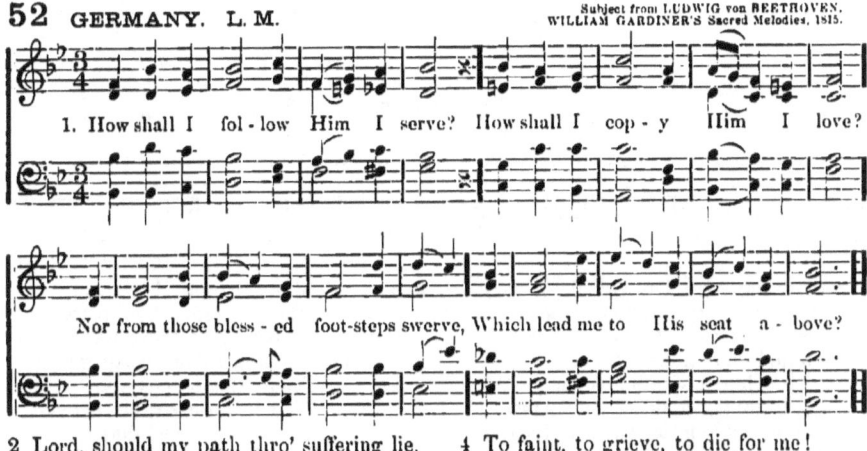

1. How shall I follow Him I serve? How shall I copy Him I love? Nor from those blessed footsteps swerve, Which lead me to His seat above?

2 Lord, should my path thro' suffering lie,
Forbid it I should e'er repine;
Still let me turn to Calvary,
Nor heed my griefs, remembering Thine.

3 Oh, let me think how Thou didst leave
Untasted every pure delight,
To fast, to faint, to watch, to grieve,
The toilsome day, the homeless night :—

4 To faint, to grieve, to die for me!
Thou camest not Thyself to please:
And, dear as earthly comforts be,
Shall I not love Thee more than these?

5 Yes! I would count them all but loss,
To gain the notice of Thine eye:
Flesh shrinks and trembles at the cross,
But Thou canst give the victory.

Josiah Conder, 1824, 1836. Ab.

BEHOLD THE MAN.

53 O AGNE DEI. L. M. D.
Rev. JAMES CARTER, 1894.

1. O Lamb of God! O Lamb of God! From loft-y, calm e-ter-ni-ty,
I see Thee tread the lone-ly road, I see Thee leave Thy throne for me.
Thy light il-lu-mines ev-'ry one With-in earth's deadliest, dark-est spot;
Thou cam-est meek un-to Thine own, And even Thine own re-ceiv'd Thee not.

Words and Music Copyright, 1894, by Rev. James Carter.

2 And all day long Thy yearning arms
   Besought reluctant men to flee
From evil ways and deadly harms,
   To find eternal rest in Thee.
All day Thine invitation sweet
   With pitying patience gently pled
That they might make Thy flesh their meat,
   Receive Thyself, their living bread.

3 And Thou hast known the look of scorn,
   The haughty scribe's imperious tones,
And sharper than the platted thorn,
   The ruin of Thy "little ones."
O Light of Light, Thy gentleness,
   Thy love, is most divine to me,
Repulsed, yet striving still to bless
   The proud and scornful Pharisee.

4 And still along the hurrying street,
   And in the thronging, busy mart,
Men with impatient, ruthless feet
   Tread on Thy patient, bleeding heart;
And yet Thine arms of pity wide
   In steadfast love their grace extend;
For, though man cavil and deride,
   Thou still wilt ever be his friend.

5 O Lamb of God! O Quenchless Love!
   As adamant our hearts must be,
If such long patience fail to move,
   And win our faithful love to Thee.
O Living Fire, consume our dross;
   Our fatal hesitance win o'er;
And lead us, captives of Thy cross,
   To life with Thee forever more.

Rev. James Carter, 1891.

THE MAN OF SORROWS.

54 ST. MARK. C. M. HENRY JOHN GAUNTLETT, 1872.

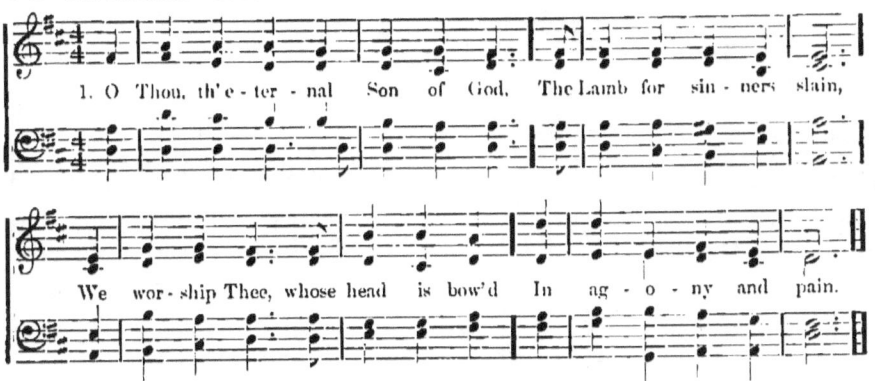

1. O Thou, th' e-ter-nal Son of God, The Lamb for sin-ners slain, We wor-ship Thee, whose head is bow'd In ag-o-ny and pain.

2 None treads with Thee Thine awful path,
  Thou sufferest alone;
  Thine is the perfect sacrifice
  Which only can atone.

3 Thou great High Priest, Thy glory robes
  To-day are laid aside;
  And human sorrows, Son of Man,
  Thy Godhead seem to hide.

4 The cross is sharp, but in Thy woe
  This is the lightest part;
  Our sin it is which pierces Thee,
  And breaks Thy sacred heart.

5 Who love Thee most, at Thy dear cross,
  Will truest, Lord, abide;
  Make Thou that cross our only hope,
  O Jesus crucified.
                William Chatterton Dix, 1864.

55 AVON. C. M. HUGH WILSON, 1825.

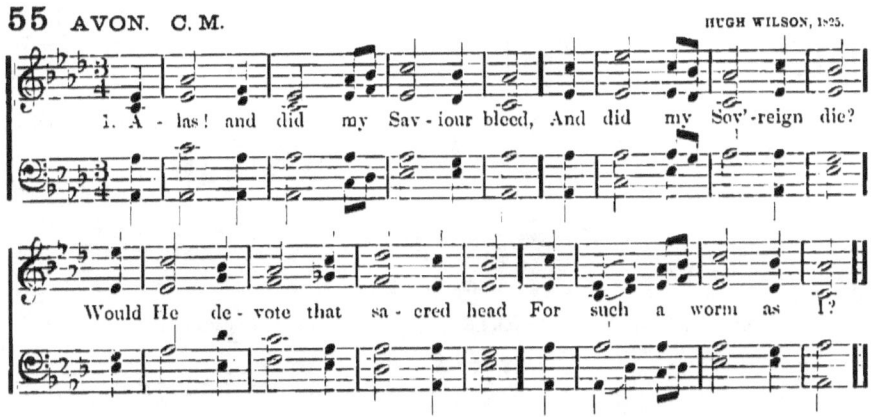

1. A-las! and did my Sav-iour bleed, And did my Sov'-reign die? Would He de-vote that sa-cred head For such a worm as I?

2 Was it for crimes that I had done
  He groaned upon the tree?
  Amazing pity! grace unknown!
  And love beyond degree!

3 Well might the sun in darkness hide,
  And shut His glories in,
  When Christ, the mighty Maker, died
  For man, the creature's sin.

4 Thus might I hide my blushing face
  While His dear cross appears;
  Dissolve my heart in thankfulness,
  And melt my eyes to tears.

5 But drops of grief can ne'er repay
  The debt of love I owe;
  Here, Lord, I give myself away,
  'Tis all that I can do.
                Rev. Isaac Watts, 1707. Ab.

DYING, AND BEHOLD HE LIVES.

56 HAMBURG. L. M.
Arr. by LOWELL MASON, 1825.

1. When I sur-vey the won-drous cross, On which the Prince of glo-ry died.
My rich-est gain I count but loss, And pour contempt on all my pride.

2 Forbid it, Lord! that I should boast,
  Save in the death of Christ, my God;
  All the vain things that charm me most,
  I sacrifice them to His blood.

3 See, from His head, His hands, His feet,
  Sorrow and love flow mingled down;
  Did e'er such love and sorrow meet,
  Or thorns compose so rich a crown?

4 His dying crimson, like a robe,
  Spreads o'er His body on the tree;
  Then I am dead to all the globe,
  And all the globe is dead to me.

5 Were the whole realm of nature mine,
  That were a present far too small;
  Love so amazing, so divine,
  Demands my soul, my life, my all.
  Rev. Isaac Watts, 1707.

57 MOZART. 7.
JOHANN C. W. A. MOZART, 1779.

1. Christ, the Lord, is ris'n to-day, Sons of men, and an-gels, say; Raise your joys and tri-umphs high! Sing, ye heav'ns, and, earth, reply! Sing, ye heav'ns, and earth, re-ply!

2 Love's redeeming work is done,
  Fought the fight, the battle won;
  Lo, our Sun's eclipse is o'er;
  Lo, He sets in blood no more.

3 Vain the stone, the watch, the seal;
  Christ hath burst the gates of hell;
  Death in vain forbids His rise;
  Christ hath opened Paradise.

4 Lives again our glorious King;
  "Where, O Death, is now thy sting?"
  Once He died our souls to save;
  "Where's thy victory, boasting Grave?"

5 Soar we now where Christ has led,
  Following our exalted Head;
  Made like Him, like Him we rise;
  Ours the cross, the grave, the skies!
  Rev. Charles Wesley, 1739. Ab.

THE LORD IS RISEN.

58 EASTER MORNING. Rev. JAMES CARTER, 1878.

1. Down from their home on high, Down thro' the star-ry sky, An-gels, de-scend-ing, fly, While the earth shak-eth; Roll they the stone a-way From where the Sav-iour lay, Out in-to glo-rious day, His way He tak-eth.

Refrain.
Loud Hal-le-lu-jahs! Loud Hal-le-lu-jahs! Our ris-en Sav-iour, to Thee we sing. Hal-le-lu-jah! Hal-le-lu-jah! Hal-le-lu-jah!

2 He from the grave is gone,
  Treading the way alone,
  Death now is overthrown
    By His endeavor.
  Where is thy victory,
  O Grave? and where shall be,
  O Death! our fear of thee?
    Perished forever.

3 Sing we Thy praise for aye,
  Who washed our sins away;
  Unto Thy name alway
    We shall be singing.
  Far down the tracts of time
  Shall every earthly clime
  Join in the song sublime,
    With praises ringing.

Rev. James Carter, 1878.

KING OF KINGS.

59 AZMON. C. M.
CARL GOTTHILF GLÄSER, 1824.
Arr. by LOWELL MASON, 1839.

1. The head that once was crown'd with thorns, Is crown'd with glo-ry now;
A roy-al di-a-dem a-dorns The might-y Vic-tor's brow.

2 The highest place that Heaven affords,
    Is His by sovereign right ;
  The King of kings, and Lord of lords,
    He reigns in glory bright ;—

3 The joy of all who dwell above,
    The joy of all below,
  To whom He manifests His love,
    And grants His Name to know.

4 To them the cross with all its shame,
    With all its grace, is given ;
  Their name—an everlasting name,
    Their joy—the joy of Heaven.

5 To them the cross is life and health,
    Though shame and death to Him ;
  His people's hope, His people's wealth,
    Their everlasting theme.

                              Rev. Thomas Kelly, 1820. Ab.

60 RUSSIA. 8.7.
ALEXIS FEODOROVITCH LWOFF, 1833.
Arr. by C. ARTHUR JACQUES, 1895.

1. Christ, a-bove all glo-ry seat-ed! King e-ter-nal, strong to save!
To Thee, Death, by death de-feat-ed, Tri-umph high and glo-ry gave.

2 Thou art gone, where now is given,
    What no mortal might could gain :
  On the eternal throne of Heaven,
    In Thy Father's power to reign.

3 There Thy kingdoms all adore Thee,
    Heaven above and earth below,
  While the depths of hell before Thee,
    Trembling and defeated bow.

4 We, O Lord ! with hearts adoring,
    Follow Thee above the sky :
  Hear our prayers Thy grace imploring,
    Lift our souls to Thee on high.

5 So when Thou again in glory
    On the clouds of Heaven shalt shine,
  We Thy flock shall stand before Thee,
    Owned forevermore as Thine.

                      Unknown Latin Writer, c. 5th. Century.
                      Bp. James Russell Woodford, 1852. Ab.

LORD OF LORDS.

61 VICTORY. 8.7.4.   HARRY HOBART BEADLE, 1854.

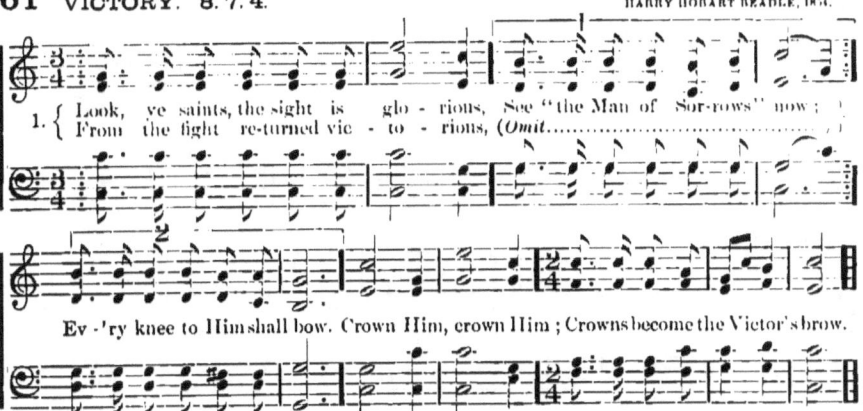

1. Look, ye saints, the sight is glorious, See "the Man of Sorrows" now;
From the fight returned victorious, (Omit)............
Ev-'ry knee to Him shall bow. Crown Him, crown Him; Crowns become the Victor's brow.

2 Crown the Saviour, angels, crown Him:
  Rich the trophies Jesus brings:
In the seat of power enthrone Him,
  While the vault of Heaven rings:
Crown Him, crown Him;
  Crown the Saviour "King of kings."

3 Sinners in derision crowned Him,
  Mocking thus the Saviour's claim;
Saints and angels crowd around Him,
  Own His title, praise His Name:
Crown Him, crown Him;
  Spread abroad the Victor's fame.

4 Hark, those bursts of acclamation!
  Hark, those loud triumphant chords!
Jesus takes the highest station:
  Oh, what joy the sight affords!
Crown Him, crown Him;
  "King of kings, and Lord of lords."
                Rev. Thomas Kelly, 1809.

62 BRADFORD. C. M.   GEORGE FREDERICK HANDEL, 1741.

1. I know that my Redeemer lives, And ever prays for me:
A token of His love He gives, A pledge of liberty.

2 I find Him lifting up my head;
  He brings salvation near:
His presence makes me free indeed,
  And He will soon appear.

3 He wills that I should holy be:
  What can withstand His will?
The counsel of His grace in me,
  He surely shall fulfill.

4 Jesus, I hang upon Thy word:
  I steadfastly believe
Thou wilt return, and claim me, Lord,
  And to Thyself receive.
               Rev. Charles Wesley, 1742. Ab.

THE HOLY SPIRIT INVOKED.

63 STEPHENS. C. M.
Rev. WILLIAM JONES, 1784.

1. Come, Ho-ly Spir-it, heav'n-ly Dove! With all Thy quick'ning pow'rs, Kin-dle a flame of sa-cred love In these cold hearts of ours.

2 Look! how we grovel here below,
   Fond of these trifling toys!
   Our souls can neither fly nor go
   To reach eternal joys.

3 In vain we tune our formal songs;
   In vain we strive to rise;
   Hosannas languish on our tongues,
   And our devotion dies.

4 Dear Lord, and shall we ever live
   At this poor, dying rate—
   Our love so faint, so cold to Thee,
   And Thine to us so great?

5 Come, Holy Spirit, heavenly Dove!
   With all Thy quickening powers;
   Come, shed abroad a Saviour's love,
   And that shall kindle ours.

Rev. Isaac Watts, 1707.

64 HAYDN. S. M.
FRANCIS JOSEPH HAYDN, 1801.

1. Come, Ho-ly Spir-it, come, Let Thy bright beams a-rise, Dis-pel the sor-row from our minds, The dark-ness from our eyes.

2 Convince us of our sin;
   Then lead to Jesus' blood,
   And to our wondering view reveal
   The mercies of our God.

3 Revive our drooping faith,
   Our doubts and fears remove,
   And kindle in our breast the flame
   Of never-dying love.

4 'Tis Thine to cleanse the heart,
   To sanctify the soul,
   To pour fresh life in every part,
   And new-create the whole.

5 Come, Holy Spirit, come;
   Our minds from bondage free;
   Then shall we know, and praise, and love,
   The Father, Son, and Thee.

Rev. Joseph Hart, 1759. Ab. and alt.

PRAYER FOR THE SPIRIT.

65 AUTUMN. 8.7. D.
FRANCOIS HIPPOLITE BARTHELEMON, c. 1796.
Arr. by ROBERT SIMPSON, 1837.

1. Love di-vine, all loves ex-cell-ing, Joy of Heav'n, to earth come down!
Fix in us Thy hum-ble dwell-ing, All Thy faith-ful mer-cies crown:
D.S.—Vis-it us with Thy sal-va-tion, En-ter ev-'ry trem-bling heart.
Je-sus! Thou art all com-pas-sion, Pure, un-bound-ed love Thou art,

2 Breathe, oh, breathe Thy loving Spirit
    Into every troubled breast!
Let us all in Thee inherit,
    Let us find Thy promised rest:
Come, Almighty to deliver,
    Let us all Thy life receive!
Speedily return, and never,
    Never more Thy temples leave!

3 Finish then Thy new creation,
    Pure, unspotted may we be:
Let us see our whole salvation
    Perfectly secured by Thee!
Changed from glory into glory,
    Till in Heaven we take our place;
Till we cast our crowns before Thee,
    Lost in wonder, love, and praise.
            Rev. Charles Wesley, 1747. Ab.

---

66 (HAYDN). S. M.

1 Lord God, the Holy Ghost!
    In this accepted hour,
As on the day of Pentecost
    Descend in all Thy power!

2 We meet with one accord
    In our appointed place,
And wait the promise of our Lord,
    The Spirit of all grace.

3 Like mighty rushing wind
    Upon the waves beneath,
Move with one impulse every mind,
    One soul, one feeling breathe.

4 The young, the old inspire
    With wisdom from above;
And give us hearts and tongues of fire
    To pray, and praise, and love.
            James Montgomery, 1825. Ab.

67 S. M.

1 O Lord, Thy work revive,
    In Zion's gloomy hour,
And make her dying graces live
    By Thy restoring power.

2 Oh, let Thy chosen few
    Awake to earnest prayer;
Their covenant again renew,
    And walk in filial fear.

3 Thy Spirit then will speak
    Through lips of humble clay,
Till hearts of adamant shall break,
    Till rebels shall obey.

4 Now lend Thy gracious ear;
    Now listen to our cry;
Oh, come and bring salvation near;
    Our souls on Thee rely.
            Phœbe Hinsdale Brown. 1819. Ab.

PRAYER FOR THE SPIRIT'S POWER.

68 PENTECOST. C. M.   Rev. JAMES CARTER, 1894.

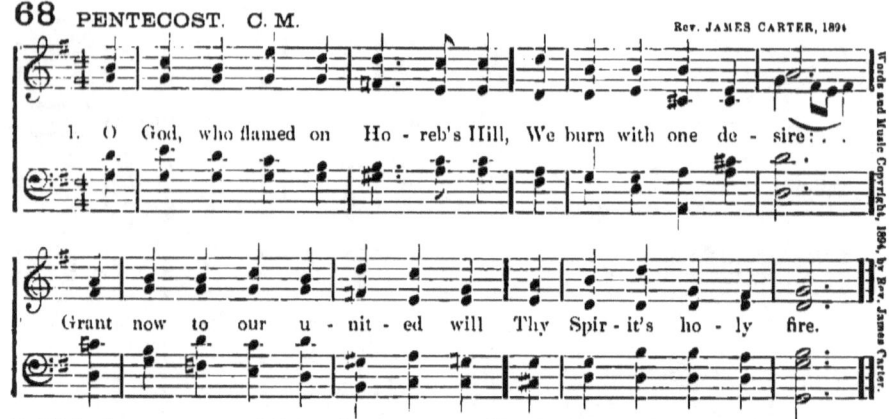

1. O God, who flamed on Horeb's Hill, We burn with one desire; Grant now to our united will Thy Spirit's holy fire.

2 With cloven tongues of living flame
   Descend on us this hour;
   Put silent witnesses to shame,
   Teach us to speak with power.

3 Grant gift of tongues, each heart to move
   In language of its own;
   Translate the message of Thy love,
   And melt the hearts of stone.

4 Touch and transform, and sweetly sway
   All spirits by Thy word;
   Grant us Thy Pentecostal day,
   Souls for Thy kingdom, Lord.

5 O God, who flamed on Horeb's Hill,
   Before Thy throne we bow;
   From Thine eternal fulness fill;
   Grant us Thy Spirit now.
                    Emma Smuller Carter, 1894.

69 HOREB. C. M.   Rev. JAMES CARTER, 1894.

1. Spirit Divine, attend our pray'rs, And make this house Thy home; Descend with all Thy gracious pow'rs, Oh, come, Great Spirit, come!

2 Come as the light; to us reveal
   Our sinfulness and woe;
   And lead us in those paths of life
   Where all the righteous go.

3 Come as the fire, and purge our hearts,
   Like sacrificial flame;
   Let our whole soul an offering be
   To our Redeemer's Name.

4 Come as the wind, with rushing sound,
   With Pentecostal grace;
   And make the great salvation known,
   Wide as the human race.

5 Spirit Divine, attend our prayers,
   Make a lost world Thy home;
   Descend with all Thy gracious powers,
   Oh, come, Great Spirit, come!
         Rev. Andrew Reed, 1819. Ab. and sl. alt.

PRAYER FOR THE SPIRIT'S POWER.

70 PETITION. 9.8. With Refrain.
Rev. JAMES CARTER, 1894.

Words and Music Copyright, 1894, by Rev. James Carter.

1. O Holy One in earth's creation Who broodedst o'er the welt'ring deeps,
Come Thou, and breathe Thine inspiration In hearts whose hidden power sleeps.

Refrain.
Heav'nly Father, hear us, At Thy throne we bow;
Come in favor near us, Grant Thy Spirit now.

2 O Breath, that bloweth where it listeth,
Thy servants wait Thy gracious sign.
Subdue in us all that resisteth
And thrill our souls with fire divine.

3 Before Thy Presence High we bow us,
Our wills we humble at Thy feet.
Oh, with Thy might divine endow us!
For faithful service make us meet.

4 We bend, and beg Thy visitation,
Unworthy we, and yet, this hour
Grant us, O Lord, the consecration
To be Thy witnesses with power.

5 Still stand we here, O Spirit Holy,
Thy soldiers waiting for their Lord;
Fill us with Thine own Self that, lowly,
We may go forth to speak Thy word.
Rev. James Carter, 1894.

71

1 Spirit Divine, who once descended,
Dove-like, upon the Saviour's head,
Now be to us Thy grace extended;
Now be on us Thy virtue shed.

REFRAIN.—Holy Spirit, bow us
To Thy blessed will;
With Thy might endow us;
With Thy wisdom fill.

2 Thou, who in Pentecostal splendor
Didst on the first disciples shine,
Come with a grace serene and tender,
Fill every soul with fire divine.

3 Give us a voice for proclamation:
Plant in our hearts Thy love so free:
Give us the power to bring salvation
Near to the souls that wait for Thee.
Rev. James Carter, 1894.
Words Copyright, 1894, by Rev. James Carter

THE WAY OF SALVATION.

72 ATHENS. C. M. D. FELICE GIARDINI, 1760.

1. I heard the voice of Jesus say, "Come unto Me and rest;
Lay down, thou weary one, lay down Thy head upon My breast."
I came to Jesus as I was, Weary, and worn, and sad;
I found in Him a resting-place, And He has made me glad.

2 I heard the voice of Jesus say,
 "Behold, I freely give
The living water; thirsty one,
 Stoop down, and drink, and live."
I came to Jesus, and I drank
 Of that life-giving stream;
My thirst was quenched, my soul revived,
 And now I live in Him.

3 I heard the voice of Jesus say,
 "I am this dark world's Light;
Look unto Me, thy morn shall rise,
 And all thy day be bright."
I looked to Jesus, and I found
 In Him my Star, my Sun;
And in that Light of life I'll walk
 Till all my journey's done.
 Rev. Horatius Bonar, 1846. Sl. alt.

73 COWPER. C. M. LOWELL MASON, 1830.

1. There is a fountain fill'd with blood Drawn from Emmanuel's veins; And sinners, plung'd beneath that flood, Lose all their guilty stains, Lose all their guilty stains.

THE WIDENESS OF SALVATION.

2 The dying thief rejoiced to see
   That fountain in his day ;
And there have I, as vile as he,
   Washed all my sins away.

3 Dear dying Lamb, Thy precious blood
   Shall never lose its power,
Till all the ransomed Church of God
   Be saved, to sin no more.

4 E'er since, by faith, I saw the stream
   Thy flowing wounds supply,
Redeeming love has been my theme,
   And shall be till I die.

5 And when this feeble, stammering tongue
   Lies silent in the grave,
Then in a nobler, sweeter song,
   I'll sing Thy power to save.

William Cowper, 1779. Ab. and alt.

74 BETHANY. 8.7. D.
HENRY SMART. 1867

1. There's a wide-ness in God's mer-cy, Like the wide-ness of the sea:
There's a kind-ness in His jus-tice, Which is more than lib-er-ty.
There is wel-come for the sin-ner, And more gra-ces for the good;
There is mer-cy with the Sav-iour; There is heal-ing in His blood.

2 There is no place where earth's sorrows
   Are more felt than up in Heaven ;
There is no place where earth's failings
   Have such kindly judgment given.
There is plentiful redemption
   In the blood that has been shed ;
There is joy for all the members
   In the sorrows of the Head.

3 For the love of God is broader
   Than the measures of man's mind ;
And the heart of the Eternal
   Is most wonderfully kind.
If our love were but more simple
   We should take Him at His word ;
And our lives would be all sunshine
   In the sweetness of our Lord.

Frederick William Faber, 1849. Ab.

THE OLD, OLD STORY.

75 I LOVE TO TELL THE STORY. 7. 6. D. With Refrain.
WILLIAM GUSTAVUS FISCHER, 1869.

1. I love to tell the Story Of un-seen things a-bove, Of Je-sus and His glo-ry, Of Je-sus and His love! I love to tell the Sto-ry! Be-cause I know it's true; It sat-is-fies my long-ings, As noth-ing else would do.

Refrain.
I love to tell the Sto-ry! 'Twill be my theme in glo-ry, To tell the Old, Old Sto-ry Of Je-sus and His love.

2 I love to tell the Story!
    More wonderful it seems,
Than all the golden fancies
    Of all our golden dreams.
I love to tell the Story!
    It did so much for me!
And that is just the reason,
    I tell it now to thee.

3 I love to tell the Story!
    'Tis pleasant to repeat
What seems, each time I tell it,
    More wonderfully sweet.
I love to tell the Story;
    For some have never heard
The message of salvation
    From God's own Holy Word.

THE LOVE OF GOD.

4 I love to tell the Story!
  For those who know it best
  Seem hungering and thirsting
  To hear it, like the rest.
  And when, in scenes of glory,
  I sing the New, New Song,
  'Twill be—the Old, Old Story
  That I have loved so long.
                    Miss Katherine Hankey, 1866.

76 WONDROUS LOVE. C. M. With Refrain. WILLIAM GUSTAVUS FISCHER, 1871.

1. God loved the world of sinners lost And ruined by the fall;
   Salvation full, at highest cost, He offers free to all.

Refrain.
Oh, 'twas love, 'twas wondrous love! The love of God to me;
It brought my Saviour from above, To die on Calvary.

2 E'en now by faith I claim Him mine,
    The risen Son of God;
  Redemption by His death I find,
    And cleansing through His blood.

3 Love brings the glorious fulness in,
    And to His saints makes known
  The blessèd rest from inbred sin,
    Through faith in Christ alone.

4 Believing souls, rejoicing go;
    There shall to you be given
  A glorious foretaste, here below,
    Of endless life in Heaven.

5 Of victory now o'er Satan's power
    Let all the ransomed sing,
  And triumph in the dying hour
    Through Christ the Lord our King.
                    Martha Matilda Stockton, 1871.

THE WAY OF SALVATION.

77 BOYLSTON. S. M.
LOWELL MASON, 1834.

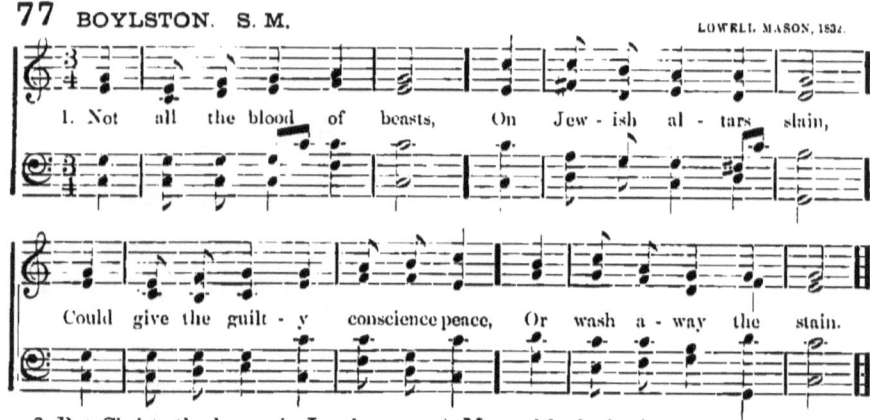

1. Not all the blood of beasts, On Jewish altars slain, Could give the guilty conscience peace, Or wash away the stain.

2 But Christ, the heavenly Lamb,
Takes all our sins away—
A sacrifice of nobler name,
And richer blood than they.

3 My faith would lay her hand
On that dear head of Thine,
While like a penitent I stand,
And there confess my sin.

4 My soul looks back to see
The burdens Thou didst bear
When hanging on the cursed tree,
And hopes her guilt was there.

5 Believing, we rejoice
To see the curse remove;
We bless the Lamb with cheerful voice,
And sing His bleeding love.

Rev. Isaac Watts, 1709.

78 MARTYN. 7. D.
SIMEON BUTLER MARSH, 1834.

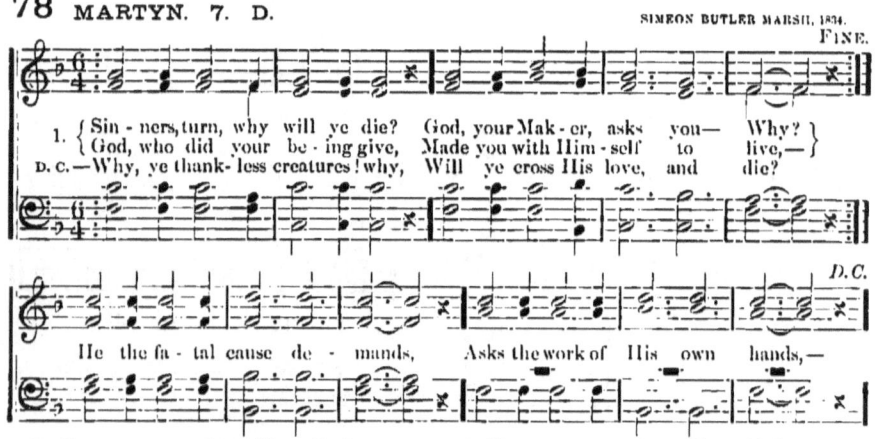

1. { Sinners, turn, why will ye die? God, your Maker, asks you—Why?
   { God, who did your being give, Made you with Himself to live,—}
D.C.—Why, ye thankless creatures! why, Will ye cross His love, and die?
He the fatal cause demands, Asks the work of His own hands,—

2 Sinners, turn, why will ye die?
God, your Saviour, asks you—Why?
He who did your souls retrieve,
Died Himself, that ye might live.
Will ye let Him die in vain?
Crucify your Lord again?
Why, ye ransomed sinners, why
Will ye slight His grace, and die?

3 Sinners, turn, why will ye die?
God, the Spirit asks you—Why?
He, who all your lives hath strove,
Urged you to embrace His love:
Will ye not His grace receive?
Will ye still refuse to live?
O ye dying sinners! why,
Why will ye forever die?

Rev. Charles Wesley, 1741. Ab.

THE ACCEPTED TIME.

79 STATE STREET. S. M. JONATHAN CALL WOODMAN, 1844.

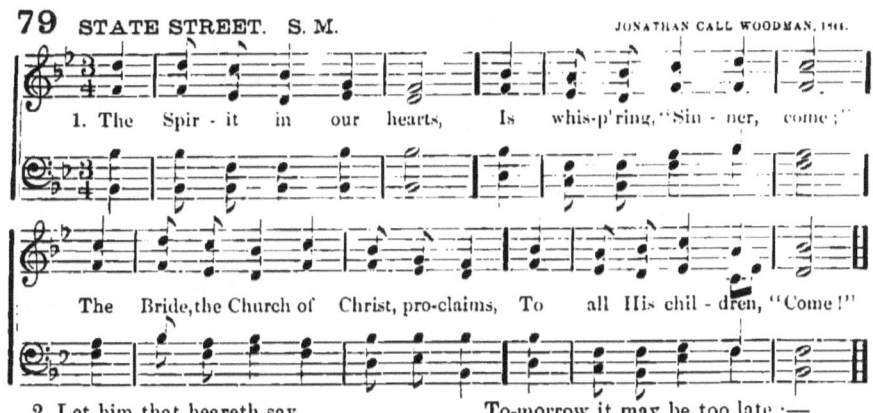

1. The Spirit in our hearts, Is whisp'ring, "Sinner, come;"
The Bride, the Church of Christ, proclaims, To all His children, "Come!"

2 Let him that heareth say
  To all about him, "Come!"
Let him that thirsts for righteousness,
  To Christ, the Fountain, come!

3 Yes, whosoever will,
  Oh! let him freely come,
And freely drink the stream of life;
  'Tis Jesus bids him come.

4 Lo! Jesus, who invites,
  Declares, "I quickly come:"
Lord, even so! we wait Thine hour;
  O blest Redeemer, come!
          Bp. Henry Ustick Onderdonk, 1826.

80
1 Now is the accepted time,
  Now is the day of grace;
O sinners! come, without delay,
  And seek the Saviour's face.

2 Now is the accepted time,
  The Saviour calls to-day;
To-morrow it may be too late;—
  Then why should you delay?

3 Now is the accepted time,
  The gospel bids you come;
And every promise, in His word,
  Declares there yet is room.
          John Dobell, 1806. Ab.

81
1 Oh, cease, my wandering soul,
  On restless wing to roam;
All this wide world, to either pole,
  Hath not for thee a home.

2 Behold the ark of God!
  Behold the open door!
Oh, haste to gain that dear abode,
  And rove, my soul, no more.

3 There safe thou shalt abide,
  There sweet shall be thy rest;
And every longing satisfied,
  With full salvation blest.
          Rev. William Augustus Muhlenburg, 1826. Ab.

82 TO-DAY. 6. 4. LOWELL MASON, 1831.

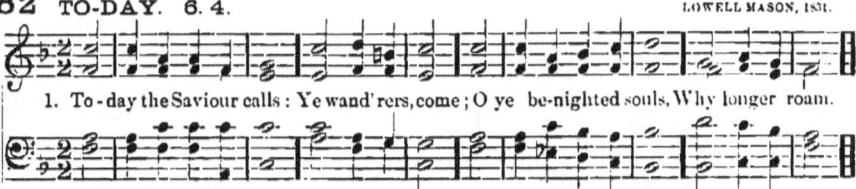

1. To-day the Saviour calls: Ye wand'rers, come; O ye benighted souls, Why longer roam.

2 To-day the Saviour calls:
  Oh, hear Him now;
Within these sacred walls
  To Jesus bow.

3 To-day the Saviour calls:
  For refuge fly;
The storm of justice falls,
  And death is nigh.

4 The Spirit calls to-day:
  Yield to His power;
Oh, grieve Him not away,
  'Tis mercy's hour.
          Rev. Samuel Francis Smith, 1831.
          Alt. by Thomas Hastings, 1831.

JESUS CALLING.

83 WHOSOEVER. 7. 6. D. With Refrain.
Rev. JAMES CARTER, 1894.

1. The voice of Christ, the Saviour, Sounds thro' the earth abroad, A voice of lov-ing fa-vor, The voice of ver-y God. The Sav-iour His sal-va-tion To all the world makes known; And this the in-vi-ta-tion He speaks in gen-tlest tone:

Refrain, Lento.
Who-so-ev-er, who-so-ev-er,—Heark-en, sin-ner, 'tis for thee.
I will not cast out,—oh, nev-er,—Him that com-eth un-to Me.

2 When life's fair morning sparkles
   With beauty and with light,
When life's still evening darkles
   In disappointment's night,
That calm, clear voice to gladness
   Securest guidance brings;
And, through the dusk of sadness,
   Invites to healing springs.

3 To all discouraged sinners
   His voice of mercy comes;
To burdened, worn bread-winners,
   To toilers in earth's homes.
When joy and beauty glisten,
   They find His way is best;
And, when the weary listen,
   His voice brings peace and rest.
     Rev. James Carter, 1894.

INVITATION.

84 ONLY A STEP.
Rev. JAMES CARTER, 1891.

Words and Music Copyright, 1893, 1894, by Rev. James Carter.

1. Only a step to Jesus! The door stands open wide. Forsake thy sin and enter in, And with thy Lord abide. This night thy soul is standing Just outside mercy's door, Oh! hear His call, trust Christ for all, And pass the threshold o'er. Only a step, only a step, Oh! take that step tonight. Only a step, only a step, From darkness into light.

2 Only a step to Jesus!
   He pleads with thee to come.
Oh! enter now, before Him bow,
   And rest in peace at home.
So near, so near to safety,
   So near the open door,—
Alas for those who see it close
   To open never more.
Only a step, only a step,
   From darkness into light.
O souls that wait at mercy's gate,
   Take, take that step to-night.

3 Only a step He asketh,
   How small a thing to do
For Him who died, the Crucified,
   For you, for you, for you.
A step to joy from sorrow,
   A step to peace from strife,
To Heaven at last, when earth is past,
   A step from death to life.
Only a step, only a step,
   Hear His sweet voice invite.
O souls that wait at mercy's gate,
   Take, take that step to-night.
                        Emma Smuller Carter, 1891.

THE FOUNTAIN OPENED.

85 FONS SALUTIS. 8.7. D. With Refrain. Rev. JAMES CARTER, 1894

1. There is a fount-ain flow-ing For earth-ly stain and sin,
E - ter-nal life be-stow-ing On those who plunge there-in.
It cleans-es from trans-gres-sion With fresh-ness ev-er bright.
Oh! come with thy con-fes-sion, And heal-ing find to-night.

Refrain. *Lento.*
Oh, come as thou art to the fountain; The path to it ev-er is free.
molto rit.
Oh, come un-to Cal-va-ry's mountain Where mer - cy is flowing for thee.

WHILE HE IS NEAR.

2 Though scarlet sins withhold thee,
   Yet for thy comfort know,
If once that flood enfold thee,
   It washes white as snow.
Not e'en thy crimson error
   That crimson fount disdains;
That blood can soothe thy terror
   And make as wool thy stains.

3 From dreams of fading splendor,
   From days of jading strife,
The Saviour's accents tender
   Invite to endless life;

Ho! every one that thirsteth;
   Come every weary soul;
The fount from Calvary bursteth
   To make the sin-sick whole.

4 O Fount of joy, Thy glory
   With deathless light doth gleam;
The saints shall hymn Thy story
   As their eternal theme.
Around the broad earth flowing
   The weary nations bless;
Till all, Thy virtue knowing,
   Thy mighty love confess.

Rev. James Carter, 1894.

86 WANDERER. 7.

Rev. JAMES CARTER, 1894.

Copyright, 1894, by Rev. James Carter.

1. Brother, hast thou wandered far From thy Father's happy home,
With thyself and God at war? Turn thee, brother; homeward come.

2 Hast thou wasted all the powers
   God for noble uses gave?
Squandered life's most golden hours?
   Turn thee, brother; God can save!

3 Is a mighty famine now
   In thy heart and in thy soul?
Discontent upon thy brow?
   Turn thee; God will make thee whole.

4 He can heal thy bitterest wound,
   He thy gentlest prayer can hear;
Seek Him, for He may be found;
   Call upon Him; He is near.

Rev. James Freeman Clarke, 1844.

87

1 Time is earnest, passing by;
   Death is earnest, drawing nigh:
Sinner, wilt thou trifling be?
   Time and death appeal to thee.

2 Life is earnest; when 'tis o'er,
   Thou returnest nevermore:
Soon to meet eternity,
   Wilt thou never serious be?

3 God is earnest; kneel and pray,
   Ere thy season pass away;
Ere He set His judgment throne;
   Ere the day of grace be gone.

4 Christ is earnest, bids thee come;
   Paid thy spirit's priceless sum;
Wilt thou spurn the Saviour's love,
   Pleading with thee from above?

5 Oh! be earnest, do not stay;
   Thou may'st perish e'en to-day.
Rise, thou lost one, rise and flee;
   Lo! thy Saviour waits for thee.

Unknown Author, 1851.

CHRIST CALLING.

88 INVITATION.
Rev. JAMES CARTER, 1894.

1. Oh, the lights are ev-er shin-ing In yon-der hap-py home,
And the door is al-ways o-pen! Oh, will you, will you come?

Refrain.
Oh, come! oh, come! The Sav-iour bids you come,
For the Fa-ther's heart is o-pen; Oh, will you, will you come?

2 By a pathway straight and narrow
The homeward journey leads;
You must leave outside its gateway
Your sinful words and deeds.

3 There is One who waits to help you,
He died on Calvary,
And His blood can cleanse your spirit
From all impurity.

4 He will gently walk beside you,
And help you on your way;
He will bear your heavy burdens,
And guide you day by day;

5 Till at last you see the shining
Of yonder happy home,
And your Saviour bids you enter;
Oh, will you, will you come?

Emma Smuller Carter, 1894.

89

1 Hark, the Shepherd's voice is calling
His wandering sheep to come,
Through the shadows gently falling:
"Come home, come home, come home."

REF.—"Come home! come home!
The night grows dark and cold.
There is warmth and light and safety
Within the sheltering fold."

2 Think, oh! think what love He bore them;
From Heaven's bright home He came,
How His heart is yearning o'er them;
He calls them all by name.

3 Where the mountain sides are steepest,
And paths are dark with sin,
Where the gloom has gathered deepest,
He calls, His sheep to win.

Emma Smuller Carter, 1894.

WARNING.

90 OSSINING. 7. 6. D.   Rev. JAMES CARTER, 1877.

Words and Music Copyright, 1894, by Rev. James Carter.

1. The message here is spoken,
The message of the Lord;
The bread of truth is broken,
The wine of love is poured.
A little while we hearken
Where lamps are burning bright;
And then, where shadows darken,
Go forth into the night.

2 How often, oh, how often
  That message has been heard
By hearts that did not soften,
  By souls that were not stirred.
A little while they tarried
  Where glowed the gospel light;
Then each his own sin carried
  Afar into the night.

3 Our sands are swiftly flowing,
  The moments flee apace;
Each human life is going
  Unto its proper place.
And when the sands are ended,
  Shall your soul take its flight
To where your life has tended,
  To find that it is night?

4 O Thou, whose arms forever
  Thy little ones enfold,
Whose patience falters never,
  Whose love is never cold,
For Jesus' merit spare us,
  Our footsteps guide aright,
May death's swift angel bear us
  Into Thy deathless light.
        Rev. James Carter, 1894.

COME.

91 AUGUSTA. 10. 8. 10. 7. With Refrain.
Rev. JAMES CARTER, 1896.

1. Hark, the voice of the Lord Jesus, calling: Ye wanderers, come unto Me. On the discords of earth it is falling, Like rain on the wind-swept sea.

Refrain.
Come to Me, come to Me, O sinner, With guilt and transgression oppressed, Come to Me, come to Me, ye weary; Oh, come, I will give you rest.

Words and Music Copyright, 1899, by Rev. James Carter.

2 Come all ye who with labor are weary,
　Come ye with your burdens distressed;
　Come ye toilers whose days have grown dreary,
　Yea, come unto Me, and rest.

3 Though the dream of your youth have been shattered,
　The hopes of your manhood all flee;
　Though you thought that to no one it mattered,
　It mattered, at least, to Me.

4 Ere the shadows of evening enfold thee,
　Life's day and its labor shall cease,
　Come to Me; with My strong arms I'll hold thee;
　Thy soul shall find rest and peace.

Rev. James Carter, 1896.

WHOSOEVER WILL.

92 EVELYN. L. M. With Refrain. Rev. JAMES CARTER, 1896.

1. Of all the words of Christ, our Lord, Of peace and par - don, Heav'n and Home, Not one is sweet - er than the word That who - so - ev - er will, may come.

Refrain.
'Tis who-so-ev - er, yes, who-so-ev - er; 'Tis who-so-ev - er will, yes, who-so-ev - er will. O sin-ner, Christ is calling thee: Come, who-so - ev - er will.

Words and Music Copyright, 1892, by Rev. James Carter.

2 Though tossed on sin's tempestuous sea,
 Though 'mid the mists of doubt thou roam,
 The voice of Jesus, calling thee,
 Saith, Whosoever will, may come.

3 Though weary of thy hopeless strife,
 Though in the Law's stern presence dumb,
 Yet He who beckons thee to life
 Saith, Whosoever will, may come.

4 No sinful soul is left without;
 He would the spacious palace fill;
 His word would place it past a doubt;
 He calleth, Whosoever will.

5 O brother, whatsoe'er the plea
 Which long hath held and holdeth still,
 The invitation is for thee;
 He calleth, Whosoever will.
   Rev. James Carter, 1896.

93

1 Oh, do not let the word depart,
 And close thine eyes against the light;
 Poor sinner, harden not thy heart:
 Thou wouldst be saved; why not to-night?

2 To-morrow's sun may never rise
 To bless thy long-deluded sight;
 This is the time; oh, then be wise!
 Thou wouldst be saved; why not to-night?

3 Our God in pity lingers still;
 And wilt thou thus His love requite?
 Renounce at length thy stubborn will;
 Thou wouldst be saved; why not to-night?

4 Our blessèd Lord refuses none
 Who would to Him their souls unite;
 Then be the work of grace begun:
 Thou wouldst be saved; why not to-night?
   Eliza Holmes Reed, 1825.

INVITATION.

94 WARFARE. 8.7. D. With Refrain.
Rev. JAMES CARTER, 1894.

1. Christ, throughout the a - ges wag-ing War that nev-er knows re-treat,
With the hosts of sin en-gag-ing, Snatch-ing vic-t'ry from de-feat,
Christ, the same to gen-er-a-tions, As from gen-er-a-tions dim,
Calm a-mid earth's pal-pi-ta-tions, Calls on you to march with Him.

Refrain.
Come then ev-'ry no-ble spir-it, Come then all the brave and strong,
Rank your-selves with right and mer-it, Stand with Christ a-gainst the wrong.

Words and Music Copyright, 1894, by Rev. James Carter.

INVITATION AND WARNING.

2 You whose consciousness of weakness
   Makes you fear to touch His hand,
Come to Jesus in your meekness;
   He will strengthen you to stand.
You whose plans have been defeated,
   Yet who long to do the right;
Christ whose conflict is completed,
   He will teach you how to fight.

3 You who see all joy before you
   From life's threshold garland-hung,
Keener pleasure may dawn o'er you
   Than the heart of man e'er sung.
March with Christ, His host victorious
   Shall advance the broad earth o'er,
Throng with shouts the City glorious,
   Reign in triumph evermore.
               Rev. James Carter, 1891.

95 NAVIGANS. 8. 6. 8. 5.
Rev. JAMES CARTER, 1894.

1. Brother, sailing o'er life's ocean, Foam beneath the prow,
Know you where your proud course tendeth? Whither sailing now?

Refrain.
Sailing, sailing onward To a distant shore,
Sailing to the harbor Whence we come no more.

2 Many a gallant ship, my brother,
   Sailing fast and far,
Never glides within the safety
   Of the harbor bar.

3 Many a gallant ship, my brother,
   Brave hearts on its deck,
By the waves of passion beaten,
   Staggers on to wreck.

4 Many a reef and many a headland,
   Shoal of treacherous sand,
Lie before your vessel's tossing
   Ere you reach the land.

5 There is One whose skillful guidance
   Never lost a crew;
Give yourself into His keeping;
   He will pilot you.
            Rev. James Carter, 1894.

THE GRACIOUS CALL.

96 HITHER. 7. 6. D. Rev. JAMES CARTER, 1894.

1. Come with your sins to Jesus, Sins that you cannot count; Come with your thirst to Jesus, Drink of the Living Fount. Come with your doubts to Jesus, Troubled and sore distress'd; Come with your toil to Jesus; Come, He will give you rest.

2 Come with your fears to Jesus,
 Fears that you cannot quell;
 Trust to the word of Jesus,
 Trust,—it will all be well.
Come with your cares to Jesus,
 Burdens you cannot bear;
Roll upon Him your burden,
 Cast upon Him your care.

3 Come with your dreary failure,
 Come with your faded dreams,
Come to the loving Shepherd,
 Come to the quiet streams.
Come as you are to Jesus,
 Ye who are sin-stained come.
Come to the Lord who leadeth
 Safe to the Father's Home.
  Rev. James Carter, 1894.

DORRNANCE. 8. 7. ISAAC BAKER WOODBURY, 1850.

1. Jesus calls us, o'er the tumult Of our life's wild, restless sea; Day by day His sweet voice sound-eth, Saying, Christian, follow Me!

REST FOR THE WEARY.

97 STEPHANOS. 8. 5. 8. 3.
Rev. Sir HENRY WILLIAM BAKER, 1868
Arr. by WILLIAM HENRY MONK, 1868

1. Art thou wea-ry, art thou lan-guid, Art thou sore dis-tressed? "Come to Me," saith One "and com-ing, Be at rest."

2 Hath He marks to lead me to Him,
    If He be my guide?
"In His feet and hands are wound-prints,
    And His side."

3 If I find Him, if I follow,
    What His guerdon here?
"Many a sorrow, many a labor,
    Many a tear."

4 If I still hold closely to Him,
    What hath He at last?
"Sorrow vanquished, labor ended,
    Jordan passed."

5 If I ask Him to receive me,
    Will He say me nay?
"Not till earth, and not till Heaven
    Pass away."

Stephen of St. Sabas, c. 750.
Tr. by Rev. John Mason Neale, 1862.

98

1 Come, thou weary, Jesus calls thee
    To His wounded side;
"Come to Me," saith He, "and ever
    Safe abide."

2 Seeking Jesus? Jesus seeks thee,—
    Wants thee as thou art;
He is knocking, ever knocking
    At thy heart.

3 Wilt thou still refuse His offer?
    Wilt thou say Him nay?
Wilt thou let Him grieved, rejected,
    Go away?

4 If thou let Him, He will save thee,—
    Make thee all His own:
Guide thee, keep thee, take thee, dying,
    To His throne.

Rev. S. C. Morgan.

99 (DORRNANCE). 8. 7.

1 Jesus calls us, o'er the tumult
    Of our life's wild, restless sea;
Day by day His sweet voice soundeth,
    Saying, Christian, follow Me!

2 Jesus calls us—from the worship
    Of the vain world's golden store;
From each idol that would keep us,—
    Saying, Christian, love Me more!

3 In our joys and in our sorrows,
    Days of toil and hours of ease,
Still He calls, in cares and pleasures,
    Christian, love Me more than these!

4 Jesus calls us! by Thy mercies,
    Saviour, may we hear Thy call;
Give our hearts to Thy obedience,
    Serve and love Thee best of all!

Cecil Frances Alexander, 1852. Ab.

100 8. 7.

1 Laboring and heavy laden
    With my sins, O Lord, I roam,
While I know Thou hast invited
    All such wanderers to their home.

2 Make my stubborn spirit willing
    To obey Thy gracious voice,
At the cross to leave its burden,
    And departing to rejoice.

3 Thy sweet yoke I'd take upon me,
    And would learn, O Lord, of Thee;
Thou art meek in heart, and lowly,
    Teach me like Thyself to be.

4 Laboring and heavy laden,
    Lord, no longer will I roam:
Here I fix my habitation,
    In Thy sheltering love at home.

Rev. Jeremiah Eames Rankin, 1855.

FOR YOU.

101 ENTREATY.
Rev. JAMES CARTER, 1896.

1. Jesus is calling to you Over the wild wastes of sin.
Through the dull sleep of death, Oh, hear what He saith, "Awaken, and let Me in."
To you, to you,
To you, to you, Tenderly calling to you.
Oh, hear Him; Oh, hark! Thro' the storm and the dark, He is calling, my brother, to you.

2 Jesus has suffered for you,
　Suffered and died on the tree.
Oh, you never can know
　That sharpness of woe
　And terrible agony.
　For you, for you,
　Lovingly suffered for you.
Shall it all be in vain?
Will you slay Him again?
　O my brother, He died for you.

3 Jesus will give unto you
　Pardon and cleansing from sin;
From your bondage release,
And fill you with peace.
　Oh, hasten, and let Him in.
　For you, for you,
　Freest forgiveness for you.
There is mercy for all,
Hear Him tenderly call,
　O my brother, to you, to you.

4 Jesus is waiting for you;
　Waiting, that heavenly Guest.
From the door of your heart
Oh, shall He depart,
　Or enter, and give you rest?
　For you, for you,
　Patiently waiting for you.
With His love and His light
He is waiting to-night,
　O my brother, for you, for you.

Emma Smuller Carter, 1895.

OUT OF DARKNESS.

102　JESUS, I COME.　　　O. R. BARROWS, 1896.

1. Out of my darkness into Thy light, Out of my weakness into Thy might; Jesus, I come, Jesus, I come; Out of my error into Thy truth, Out of my guessing into Thy sooth, Out of my sickness into Thy youth, Jesus, I come, Jesus, I come.

2 Out of my bondage and sorrow and strife,
　Into Thy freedom, forgiveness and life;
　　Jesus, I come, Jesus, I come;
　Out of unrest to breathing Thy balm,
　Out of my tumult into Thy calm,
　Out of my woes to song and to psalm,
　　Jesus, I come, Jesus, I come.

3 Out of death's horrors and madness and chains,
　Into life's comforts and glories and gains;
　　Jesus, I come, Jesus, I come;
　Out of sin's guilt and terror and gloom,
　Out of the region and shade of the tomb,
　Here where the lost still find there is room,
　　Jesus, I come, Jesus, I come.

4 Out of my pride and perverseness of will,
　Free from that void Thou only canst fill,
　　Jesus, I come, Jesus, I come;
　Out of my will, my Sovereign to own,
　Trusting Thy merits, Jesus alone,—
　Lately so lost, to crown and to throne,
　　Jesus, I come, Jesus, I come.
　　　　　Rev. Jeremiah Eames Rankin, 1896.

CHOOSING CHRIST.

103 WHITAKER. 8. 7. D.
FRIEDRICH FREIHERR VON FLOTOW, 1847.
Arr. by C. ARTHUR JACQUES, 1894.

1. Jesus, I my cross have taken, All to leave and follow Thee:
Naked, poor, despised, forsaken, Thou, from hence, my all shalt be!
D.S.—rich is my condition, God and Heav'n are still my own!
Perish, ev'ry fond ambition, All I've sought, or hoped, or known, Yet how

2 Man may trouble and distress me,
  'Twill but drive me to Thy breast,
Life with trials hard may press me,
  Heaven will bring me sweeter rest.
Oh! 'tis not in grief to harm me,
  While Thy love is left to me;
Oh! 'twere not in joy to charm me,
  Were that joy unmixed with Thee.

3 Go then, earthly fame and treasure!
  Come disaster, scorn, and pain!
In Thy service pain is pleasure,
  With Thy favor, loss is gain.
I have called Thee, Abba, Father!
  I have stayed my heart on Thee!
Storms may howl, and clouds may gather,
  All must work for good to me.

4 Let the world despise and leave me,
  They have left my Saviour, too;
Human hearts and looks deceive me;
  Thou art not, like them, untrue;
Oh! while Thou dost smile upon me,
  God of wisdom, love, and might,
Foes may hate, and friends disown me,
  Show Thy face, and all is bright.
      Rev. Henry Francis Lyte, 1824. Ab.

104

1 Take me, O my Father, take me!
  Take me, save me, through Thy Son;
That which Thou wouldst have me, make
  Let Thy will in me be done. [me,
Long from Thee my footsteps straying,
  Thorny proved the way I trod;
Weary come I now, and praying—
  Take me to Thy love, my God!

2 Fruitless years with grief recalling,
  Humbly I confess my sin;
At Thy feet, O Father, falling,
  To Thy household take me in.
Freely now to Thee I proffer
  This relenting heart of mine;
Freely life and soul I offer—
  Gift unworthy love like Thine.

3 Once the world's Redeemer, dying,
  Bare our sins upon the tree;
On that sacrifice relying,
  Now I look in hope to Thee;
Father, take me! all forgiving,
  Fold me to Thy loving breast;
In Thy love for ever living,
  I must be for ever blest!
      Rev. Ray Palmer, 1864. Ab.

105 PALMER.

HORATIO RICHMOND PALMER, c. 1870

Used by permission of Dr H. R. Palmer, owner of Copyright.

1. Hark! the voice of Jesus calling, "Follow Me, follow Me!"
Softly through the silence falling, "Follow, follow Me!"
As of old He called the fishers, When He walked by Galilee,
Still His patient voice is pleading, "Follow, follow Me!"

2 Who will heed the holy mandate,
   "Follow Me, follow Me!"
Leaving all things at His bidding,
   "Follow, follow Me!"
Hark! that tender voice entreating
Mariners on life's rough sea,
Gently, lovingly, repeating,
   "Follow, follow Me!"

3 Hearken, lest He plead no longer,
   "Follow Me, follow Me!"
Once again, oh, hear Him calling,
   "Follow, follow Me!"
Turning swift at Thy sweet summons,
Evermore, O Christ, would we,
For Thy love all else forsaking,
Follow, follow Thee!

Miss Mary B. Sleight, c. 1870.

106 (WHITAKER). 8. 7. D.

1 Take my heart, O Father! take it;
   Make and keep it all Thine own;
Let Thy Spirit melt and break it—
   This proud heart of sin and stone.
Father, make me pure and lowly,
   Fond of peace and far from strife;
Turning from the paths unholy
   Of this vain and sinful life.

2 Ever let Thy grace surround me,
   Strengthen me with power divine,
Till Thy cords of love have bound me:
   Make me to be wholly Thine.
May the blood of Jesus heal me,
   And my sins be all forgiven;
Holy Spirit, take and seal me,
   Guide me in the path to Heaven.

Unknown Writer, 1849.

COMING TO GOD.

107 WOODWORTH. L. M.   WILLIAM BATCHELDER BRADBURY, 1849.

2 Just as I am, and waiting not
   To rid my soul of one dark blot, [spot,
   To Thee, whose blood can cleanse each
      O Lamb of God, I come.

3 Just as I am, though tossed about
   With many a conflict, many a doubt,
   By fears within and foes without,
      O Lamb of God, I come.

. Just as I am, Thou wilt receive,
   Wilt welcome, pardon, cleanse, relieve ;
   Because Thy promise I believe,
      O Lamb of God, I come.

5 Just as I am, Thy love unknown
   Has broken every barrier down :
   Now, to be Thine, yea, Thine alone,
      O Lamb of God, I come.
                Miss Charlotte Elliott, 1836. Ab. and sl. alt.

108

1 God calling yet ! shall I not hear ?
   Earth's pleasures shall I still hold dear ?
   Shall life's swift passing years all fly,
   And still my soul in slumber lie ?

2 God calling yet ! and shall He knock,
   And I my heart the closer lock ?
   He still is waiting to receive,
   And shall I dare His Spirit grieve ?

3 God calling yet ! and shall I give
   No heed, and still in bondage live ?
   I wait, but He does not forsake ;
   He calls me still ; my heart, awake !

4 God calling yet ! I cannot stay,
   My heart I yield without delay ;
   Vain world, farewell from thee I part ;
   The voice of God hath reached my heart.
                Rev. Gerhard Tersteegen, 1735.
                Tr. by Sarah Findlater, 1855. Ab. and alt.

ALMSGIVING. 8. 8. 8. 4.   Rev. JOHN BACCHUS DYKES, 1875.

COMING TO THE CROSS.

109 TRUSTING. 7. WILLIAM GUSTAVUS FISCHER, 1869.

1. I am coming to the cross; I am poor, and weak, and blind;
Ref.—I am trusting, Lord, in Thee, Dear Lamb of Calvary;
I am counting all but dross; I shall full salvation find.
Humbly at Thy cross I bow; Save me, Jesus, save me now.

2 Here I give my all to Thee,
  Friends and time and earthly store;
  Soul and body Thine to be,
  Wholly Thine for evermore.

3 In the promises I trust;
  Now I feel the blood applied;
  I am prostrate in the dust;
  I with Christ am crucified.
  Rev. William McDonald, 1858. Ab.

110 ST. HELEN'S. 8.5.8.3. ROBERT PRESCOTT STEWART, 1874.

1. I am trusting Thee, Lord Jesus, Trusting only Thee! Trusting
Thee for full salvation, Great and free.

2 I am trusting Thee for pardon,
  At Thy feet I bow;
  For Thy grace and tender mercy,
  Trusting now.

3 I am trusting Thee for cleansing
  In the crimson flood;
  Trusting Thee to make me holy
  By Thy blood.

4 I am trusting Thee to guide me;
  Thou alone shalt lead,
  Every day and hour supplying
  All my need.

5 I am trusting Thee, Lord Jesus;
  Never let me fall;
  I am trusting Thee for ever,
  And for all.
  Miss Frances Ridley Havergal, 1874. Ab.

111 (ALMSGIVING). 8.8.8.4.

1 God of my life! Thy boundless grace
  Chose, pardoned, and adopted me;
  My Rest, my Home, my Dwelling-place;
  I come to Thee.

2 Jesus, my Hope, my Rock, my Shield!
  Whose precious blood was shed for me,
  Into Thy hands my soul I yield;
  I come to Thee.

3 Spirit of glory and of God!
  Long hast Thou deigned my guide to be;
  Now be Thy comfort sweet bestowed;
  I come to Thee.

4 I come to join that countless host,
  Who praise Thy Name unceasingly;
  Blest Father, Son, and Holy Ghost!
  I come to Thee.
  Miss Charlotte Elliott, 1841.

TURNING TO CHRIST.

112 SUBMISSION. 7. 6 l.
Emma Smuller Carter, 1894.
Arr. by Rev. James Carter, 1894.

1. Je-sus, Lord, I turn to Thee;
Thou hast wait-ed long for me.
Me Thy pre-cious blood has bought;
Me Thy pa-tient love has sought.
Now, at last, that love I see;
Je-sus, Lord, I turn to Thee.

2 Pardon, Lord, Thy willful child,
Stubborn, selfish, sin-defiled;
Wayward, wandering from Thy fold;
Lost upon the mountains cold.
Tenderly Thou callest me;
Jesus, Lord, I turn to Thee.

3 Take me, Saviour, to Thy breast;
Give me shelter, give me rest.
Safe with Thee I would abide;
Keep me ever near Thy side;
Pardon, cleanse, and strengthen me.
Jesus, Lord, I turn to Thee.

4 When temptations come again,
May I fear to give Thee pain;
When I stumble in the way,
Hold me fast, dear Lord, I pray.
To none other can I flee;
Jesus, Lord, I turn to Thee.

5 All Thine own Thou dost defend;
Thou wilt keep them to the end.
Now, O Lord, for life or death,
I would look to Thee in faith;
Now, and for eternity,
Jesus, Lord, I turn to Thee.

Emma Smuller Carter, 1894.

113 (TOPLADY).

1 Rock of Ages, cleft for me!
Let me hide myself in Thee;
Let the water and the blood,
From Thy wounded side that flowed,
Be of sin the double cure;
Cleanse me from its guilt and power.

2 Not the labor of my hands
Can fulfill the law's demands;
Could my zeal no respite know,
Could my tears forever flow,
All for sin could not atone,
Thou must save, and Thou alone.

3 Nothing in my hand I bring,
Simply to Thy cross I cling;
Naked, come to Thee for dress,
Helpless, look to Thee for grace;
Foul, I to the fountain fly,
Wash me, Saviour, or I die!

4 While I draw this fleeting breath,
When my eyelids close in death,
When I soar to worlds unknown,
See Thee on Thy judgment-throne,
Rock of Ages, cleft for me!
Let me hide myself in Thee.

Rev. Augustus Montague Toplady, 1776.

AT THE GATE.

114 PENITENCE. 7. 6 l. Rev. JAMES CARTER, 1894.

1. Jesus, Saviour, sick of sin, I am kneeling at the gate. Now in mercy take me in; Save me ere it be too late. Friend of sinners, pierced for me, Only Thou my refuge be.

2 From Thy way I've wandered far ;
　Far from peace and safety gone ;
　Marked with many a stain and scar,
　Now I seek Thy cross alone.
　Friend of sinners, pierced for me,
　Only Thou my refuge be.

3 All the years Thy tenderness
　Touched my heart, while I refused ;
　While Thy patience strove to bless,
　I that patience still abused.
　Friend of sinners, pierced for me,
　Only Thou my refuge be.

4 Nothing have I of excuse ;
　Nothing worthy I possess,
　Naught of value or of use,
　Nothing save my sinfulness.
　Friend of sinners, pierced for me,
　Only Thou my refuge be.

5 So I come to Thee, O Lord,
　Weary of the endless strife,
　Pleading but Thy faithful word,
　Pleading for my forfeit life.
　Friend of sinners, pierced for me,
　Only Thou my refuge be.

6 Saviour, I Thy grace implore :
　Burdened with my load of sin,
　I am kneeling at the door ;
　Open, Lord, and take me in.
　Friend of sinners, pierced for me,
　Only Thou my refuge be.

　　　　　Rev. James Carter, 1894.

TOPLADY. 7. 6 l. THOMAS HASTINGS, 1830.

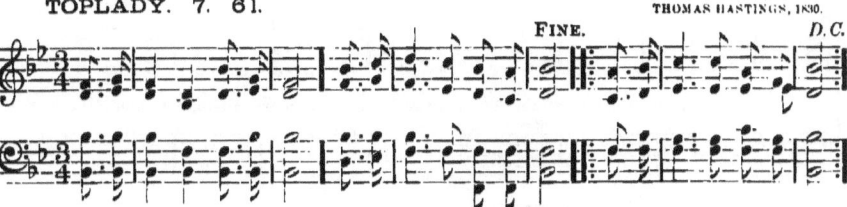

AT THE DOOR.

115 ST. HILDA. 7.6. D.
JUSTIN HEINRICH KNECHT, 1793.
Rev. EDWARD HUSBAND, 1871.

1. O Jesus, Thou art standing Outside the fast closed door,
In lowly patience waiting To pass the threshold o'er.
Shame on us, Christian brethren; His name and sign who bear,
Oh, shame, thrice shame upon us, To keep Him standing there!

2 O Jesus, Thou art knocking:
And lo, that hand is scarred,
And thorns Thy brow encircle,
And tears Thy face have marred.
Oh, love that passeth knowledge,
So patiently to wait!
Oh, sin that hath no equal,
So fast to bar the gate!

3 O Jesus, Thou art pleading
In accents meek and low,
"I died for you, My children,
And will ye treat Me so?"
O Lord, with shame and sorrow
We open now the door:
Dear Saviour, enter, enter,
And leave us never more.

Bp. William Walsham How, 1867.

VENIO. 5. 4.
Rev. JAMES CARTER, 1896.

Saviour, for refuge Come I to Thee, For Thou art calling Sinners like me.

Words and Music Copyright, 1899, by Rev. James Carter.

SALVATION SOUGHT.

116 SUPPLICATION. 9. 6. With Refrain. Rev. JAMES CARTER, 1894.

1. Soft, as they list, the airs of heav-en Now move from tree to tree.
Oh, move our hearts this ho-ly ev-en, Lord, as we kneel to Thee.

Refrain.
Ho-ly Spir-it, now de-scend-ing, Breathe Thy bless-ing as we bow:
Fill our hearts with love un-end-ing, Wake to life e-ter-nal now.

Words and Music Copyright, 1894, by Rev. James Carter.

2 Sway, as the pliant boughs are swaying,
   Each stubborn, willful soul,
  Teach us to yield, while we are praying,
   Our hearts to Thy control.

3 Turn not from us, O Spirit Holy;
   Though oft we turn astray.

Come, as our hearts are bending lowly,
  And teach us how to pray.

4 Cover with clouds of deep contrition,
   For sins that mar our years;
  Then smile with promise of remission
   And span with hope our tears.
     Emma Smuller Carter, 1894.

117 (VENIO). 5. 4.

1 Saviour, for refuge
   Come I to Thee,
  For Thou art calling
   Sinners like me.

2 Lord, Thou has promised;
   How can I doubt?
  Not one who cometh
   Wilt Thou cast out.

3 No plea I offer,
   Only my sin;

Here stand I, knocking;
   Lord, take me in.

4 Fettered by Satan,
   Come I to Thee;
  Speak but the word, Lord;
   Thy suppliant free.

5 How can I combat
   Love so divine?
  King, claim Thy captive;
   Lord, I am Thine!
     Rev. James Carter, 1896.

CLINGING TO THE CRUCIFIED.

118 JESUS MIHI MORITUR. Rev. JAMES CARTER. 1896.

1. Christ, for sinners crucified, This my only plea: Since for sinners Thou hast died, Thou hast died for me. Clinging to the Crucified, This my only plea: I will trust in none beside; Jesus died for me.

2 I no other fitness have;
    This my claim must be:
Jesus died the lost to save,
    Jesus died for me.

3 Thou hast waited at my door,
    Oh! so patiently,
Gently saying o'er and o'er,
    "Child, I died for thee."

4 Now before Thy door, O Lord,
    Me a suppliant see,
Pleading but that gracious word,
    Jesus died for me.

5 Pleading, trembling 'neath my sin,
    Oh! how tenderly
Thou dost say: "Come, enter in;
    Love, and live for Me."

Emma Smuller Carter, 1896.

---

119 (OLIVET). 6. 6. 4. 6. 6. 6. 4.

1 My faith looks up to Thee,
    Thou Lamb of Calvary,
        Saviour divine!
Now hear me while I pray,
Take all my guilt away,
Oh, let me from this day
        Be wholly Thine!

2 May Thy rich grace impart
    Strength to my fainting heart;
        My zeal inspire;
As Thou hast died for me,
Oh, may my love to Thee
Pure, warm, and changeless be,
        A living fire.

3 While life's dark maze I tread,
    And griefs around me spread,
        Be Thou my guide;
Bid darkness turn to day,
Wipe sorrow's tears away,
Nor let me ever stray
        From Thee aside.

4 When ends life's transient dream,
    When death's cold sullen stream
        Shall o'er me roll,
Blest Saviour! then, in love,
Fear and distrust remove;
Oh, bear me safe above,
        A ransomed soul!

Rev. Ray Palmer, 1830.

CHRIST OUR GLORY.

121 FEDERAL STREET. L. M. HENRY KEMBLE OLIVER, 1832.

1. Je-sus! and shall it ev-er be, A mor-tal man a-shamed of Thee?
A-shamed of Thee, whom an-gels praise, Whose glo-ries shine thro' end-less days.

2 Ashamed of Jesus! sooner far
Let evening blush to own a star;
He sheds the beams of light divine
O'er this benighted soul of mine.

3 Ashamed of Jesus! that dear Friend
On whom my hopes of Heaven depend!
No; when I blush—be this my shame,
That I no more revere His Name.

4 Ashamed of Jesus! yes, I may,
When I've no guilt to wash away;
No tear to wipe, no good to crave,
No fears to quell, no soul to save.

5 Till then—nor is my boasting vain—
Till then I boast a Saviour slain!
And oh, may this my glory be,
That Christ is not ashamed of me!

Rev. Joseph Grigg, 1765. Ab. and alt.
Rev. Benjamin Francis, 1787.

122 ORTONVILLE. C. M. THOMAS HASTINGS, 1837.

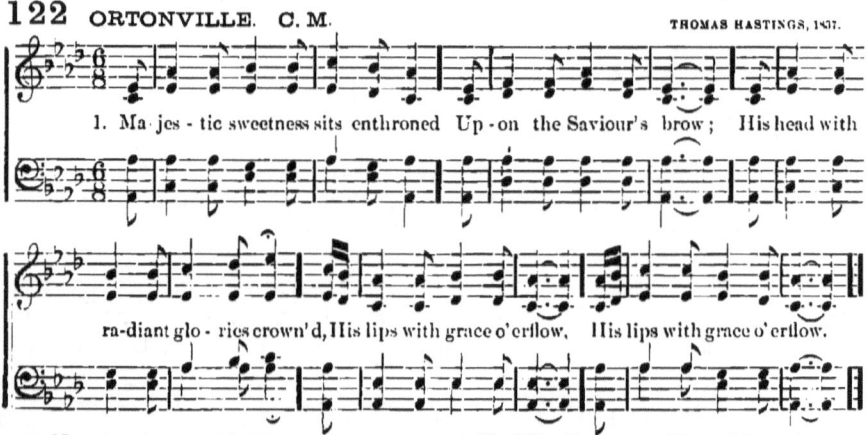

1. Ma-jes-tic sweetness sits enthroned Up-on the Saviour's brow; His head with
ra-diant glo-ries crown'd, His lips with grace o'erflow. His lips with grace o'erflow.

2 No mortal can with Him compare,
Among the sons of men;
Fairer is He than all the fair
That fill the heavenly train.

3 He saw me plunged in deep distress,
He flew to my relief;
For me He bore the shameful cross,
And carried all my grief.

4 To Him I owe my life and breath,
And all the joys I have;
He makes me triumph over death,
He saves me from the grave.

5 Since from His bounty I receive
Such proofs of love divine,
Had I a thousand hearts to give,
Lord! they should all be Thine.

Rev. Samuel Stennett, 1787. Ab.

123 HEBER. C. M. — GEORGE KINGSLEY

1. How sweet the Name of Jesus sounds In a believer's ear! It soothes his sorrows, heals his wounds, And drives away his fear.

2 It makes the wounded spirit whole,
　And calms the troubled breast;
　'Tis manna to the hungry soul,
　And to the weary, rest.

3 Jesus! my Shepherd, Guardian, Friend,
　My Prophet, Priest, and King;
　My Lord, my Life, my Way, my End,
　Accept the praise I bring.

4 Weak is the effort of my heart,
　And cold my warmest thought;
　But when I see Thee as Thou art,
　I'll praise Thee as I ought.

5 Till then I would Thy love proclaim,
　With every fleeting breath;
　And may the music of Thy Name,
　Refresh my soul in death.
　　　　Rev. John Newton, 1779. V. 3 sl. alt.

124

1 My God, accept my heart this day,
　And make it always Thine;
　That I from Thee no more may stray,
　No more from Thee decline.

2 Before the cross of Him who died,
　Behold, I prostrate fall;
　Let every sin be crucified,
　Let Christ be all in all.

3 Let every thought, and work, and word
　To Thee be ever given;
　Then life shall be Thy service Lord,
　And death the gate of Heaven!
　　　　Matthew Bridges, 1848. Ab.

125

1 Jesus, the very thought of Thee,
　With sweetness fills my breast:
　But sweeter far Thy face to see,
　And in Thy presence rest.

2 Nor voice can sing, nor heart can frame,
　Nor can the memory find
　A sweeter sound than Thy blest Name,
　O Saviour of mankind!

3 O Hope of every contrite heart!
　O Joy of all the meek!
　To those who fall, how kind Thou art!
　How good to those who seek!

4 But what to those who find? Ah! this,
　Nor tongue nor pen can show,
　The love of Jesus, what it is,
　None but His loved ones know.

5 Jesus, our only joy be Thou,
　As Thou our prize wilt be;
　Jesus, be Thou our glory now,
　And through eternity.
　　　　Bernard of Clairvaux, c. 1150.
　　　　Tr. by Rev. Edward Caswall, 1849.

ST. AGNES. C. M. — Rev. JOHN BACCHUS DYKES, 1858.

THE PRAISE OF CHRIST.

126 ARIEL. C. P. M. JOHANN C. W. A. MOZART.
LOWELL MASON, 1836.

1. Oh, could I speak the matchless worth, Oh, could I sound the glories forth, Which in my Saviour shine! I'd soar, and touch the heav'nly strings, And vie with Gabriel, while he sings In notes al-most di-vine, In notes al-most di-vine.

2 I'd sing the precious blood He spilt,
My ransom from the dreadful guilt,
Of sin and wrath divine!
I'd sing His glorious righteousness,
In which all-perfect heavenly dress
My soul shall ever shine.

3 I'd sing the characters He bears,
And all the forms of love He wears,
Exalted on His throne;
In loftiest songs of sweetest praise,
I would to everlasting days
Make all His glories known.

4 Well—the delightful day will come,
When my dear Lord will bring me home,
And I shall see His face:
Then with my Saviour, Brother, Friend,
A blest eternity I'll spend,
Triumphant in His grace.

Rev. Samuel Medley, 1789. Ab.

CHESTERFIELD. C. M. Rev. THOMAS HAWEIS, 1792.

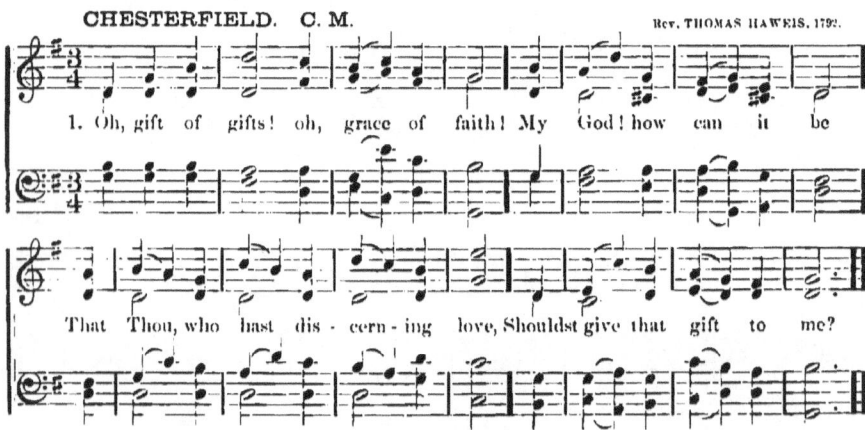

1. Oh, gift of gifts! oh, grace of faith! My God! how can it be That Thou, who hast discerning love, Shouldst give that gift to me?

127 STOWE. 11. 10. Rev. JAMES CARTER, 1899.

1. We would see Jesus, for the shadows lengthen Across this little landscape of our life; We would see Jesus our weak faith to strengthen, For the last weariness, the final strife.

2 We would see Jesus,—the great Rock Foundation,
Whereon our feet were set by sovereign grace;
Not life, nor death, with all their agitation,
Can thence remove us, if we see His face.

3 We would see Jesus;—this is all we're needing,
Strength, joy and willingness come with the sight;
We would see Jesus, dying, risen, pleading;
Then welcome day, and farewell mortal night!

Unknown Writer, 1858. Ab.

---

128 (CHESTERFIELD). C. M.

1 Oh, gift of gifts! oh, grace of faith!
  My God! how can it be
That Thou, who hast discerning love,
  Shouldst give that gift to me?

2 Ah, Grace! into unlikeliest hearts
  It is thy boast to come,
The glory of thy light to find
  In darkest spots a home.

3 The crowd of cares, the weightiest cross,
  Seem trifles less than light—
Earth looks so little and so low
  When faith shines full and bright.

4 Oh, happy, happy that I am!
  If thou canst be, O Faith,
The treasure that thou art in life,
  What wilt thou be in death!

Rev. Frederick William Faber, 1849. Ab.

129 C. M.

1 Oh! for a thousand tongues to sing
  My dear Redeemer's praise!
The glories of my God and King,
  The triumphs of His grace!

2 My gracious Master and my God!
  Assist me to proclaim,
To spread, through all the earth abroad,
  The honors of Thy Name.

3 Jesus,—the Name that calms my fears,
  That bids my sorrows cease;
'Tis music to my ravished ears;
  'Tis life, and health, and peace.

4 He breaks the power of reigning sin,
  He sets the prisoner free;
His blood can make the foulest clean;
  His blood availed for me.

Rev. Charles Wesley, 1738. Ab.

LONGING FOR CHRIST.

130 ASPIRATION. C. M. D. Rev. JAMES CARTER, 1894.

1. Jesus, my Lord, how oft I long, If such a thing could be,
For one sweet hour to join the throng That followed after Thee,
For one sweet hour to see the pow'r That made the blind to see,
To hear Thee teach from tree or flow'r, And follow after Thee.

2 The lame, the blind, to be with them,
  What joy were that to me,
If I might touch Thy garment's hem,
  And follow after Thee.
Yet, Lord, if I am leading such,
  Blind souls that seek to see,
Near to Thy helping, healing touch,
  I follow after Thee.

3 If, answering my prayer, Thy word
  Some captive soul set free ;
Do not I walk with them, O Lord,
  Who follow after Thee ?
With joy I'll serve, with joy I'll sing,
  Till I some day shall see
Thy look of love, my Lord, my King,
  And ever dwell with Thee.
            Emma Smuller Carter, 1894.

131

1 Talk with me, Lord, Thyself reveal,
    While here on earth I rove ;
  Speak to my heart, and let me feel
    The kindling of Thy love.
  With Thee conversing, I forget
    All time and toil and care ;
  Labor is rest, and pain is sweet,
    If Thou, my God, art here.

2 Thou callest me to seek Thy face ;
    Thy face, O God, I seek,—
  Attend the whispers of Thy grace,
    And hear Thee inly speak.
  Let this my every hour employ,
    Till I Thy glory see,
  Enter into my Master's joy,
    And find my Heaven in Thee.
                Rev. Charles Wesley, 1740.

STEPS TO HEAVEN.

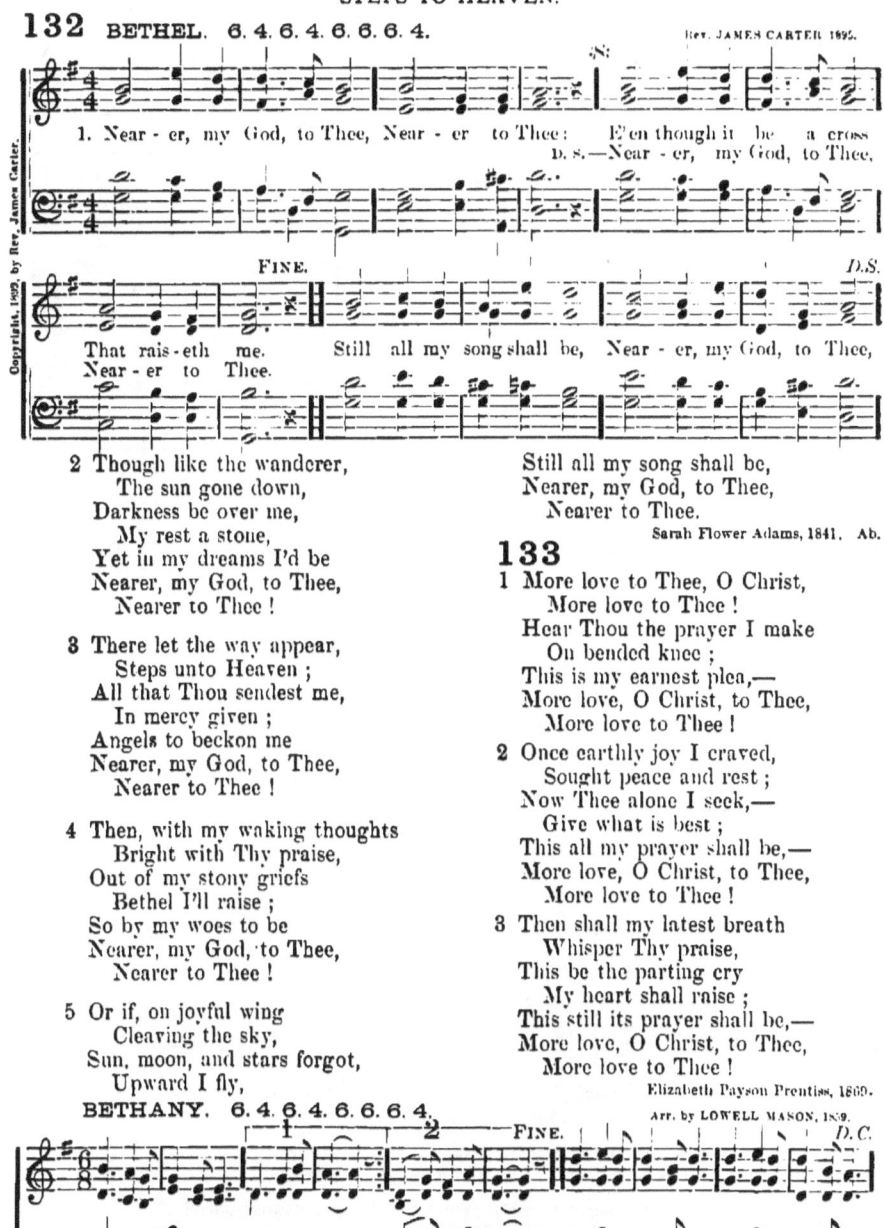

132 BETHEL. 6. 4. 6. 4. 6. 6. 6. 4. Rev. JAMES CARTER 1895.

1. Near-er, my God, to Thee, Near-er to Thee: E'en though it be a cross
D. S.—Near-er, my God, to Thee.
That rais-eth me. Still all my song shall be, Near-er, my God, to Thee,
Near-er to Thee.

2 Though like the wanderer,
  The sun gone down,
  Darkness be over me,
  My rest a stone,
Yet in my dreams I'd be
Nearer, my God, to Thee,
  Nearer to Thee !

3 There let the way appear,
  Steps unto Heaven ;
  All that Thou sendest me,
  In mercy given ;
Angels to beckon me
Nearer, my God, to Thee,
  Nearer to Thee !

4 Then, with my waking thoughts
  Bright with Thy praise,
  Out of my stony griefs
  Bethel I'll raise ;
So by my woes to be
Nearer, my God, to Thee,
  Nearer to Thee !

5 Or if, on joyful wing
  Cleaving the sky,
  Sun, moon, and stars forgot,
  Upward I fly,
  Still all my song shall be,
Nearer, my God, to Thee,
  Nearer to Thee.
  Sarah Flower Adams, 1841. Ab.

133
1 More love to Thee, O Christ,
    More love to Thee !
  Hear Thou the prayer I make
    On bended knee ;
  This is my earnest plea,—
  More love, O Christ, to Thee,
    More love to Thee !

2 Once earthly joy I craved,
    Sought peace and rest ;
  Now Thee alone I seek,—
    Give what is best ;
  This all my prayer shall be,—
  More love, O Christ, to Thee,
    More love to Thee !

3 Then shall my latest breath
    Whisper Thy praise,
  This be the parting cry
    My heart shall raise ;
  This still its prayer shall be,—
  More love, O Christ, to Thee,
    More love to Thee !
    Elizabeth Payson Prentiss, 1869.

BETHANY. 6. 4. 6. 4. 6. 6. 6. 4. Arr. by LOWELL MASON, 1859.

Used by arrangement with Oliver Ditson Company, owners of the Copyright.

THE EVERLASTING ARMS.

134 WILTWYCK. 11. 10. 11. 6. Rev. JAMES CARTER, 1897.

1. Of all the thoughts which days of old bequeath Thee, What more than this the troubled spirit charms: God is thine ageless refuge, and beneath thee His everlasting arms.

2 Rest, weary one, on Jesus' bosom leaning,
   There safe abide secure from all alarms.
Sweet is the trust that learns the secret meaning,
   In everlasting arms.

3 Peace, warring heart, 'mid earth's discordant noises;
   Firm is thy fortress safe from all that harms.
List to the quiet of the heavenly voices,
   In everlasting arms.
          Rev. James Carter, 1897.

135 PAX TECUM. 10. 21. Rev. G. T. CALDBECK, 1878.

1. Peace, perfect peace, in this dark world of sin? The blood of Jesus whispers peace within.

2 Peace, perfect peace, with loved ones far away?
   In Jesus' keeping we are safe and they.

3 Peace, perfect peace, our future all unknown?
   Jesus we know, and He is on the throne.

4 Peace, perfect peace, death shadowing us and ours?
   Jesus has vanquished death and all its powers.

5 It is enough: earth's struggles soon shall cease,
   And Jesus call us to Heaven's perfect peace.
          Bp. Edward Henry Bickersteth, 1875. Ab.

THE ONE THING NEEDFUL.

136 ESHTEMOA. 7. TIMOTHY BATTLE MASON, 1852.

1. Blessèd fountain, full of grace! Grace for sinners, grace for me, To this source alone I trace What I am and hope to be.

2 What I am, as one redeemed,
  Saved and rescued by the Lord;
  Hating what I once esteemed,
  Loving what I once abhorred.

3 What I hope to be ere long,
  When I take my place above;
  When I join the heavenly throng;
  When I see the God of love.

4 Then I hope like Him to be,
  Who redeemed His saints from sin,
  Whom I now obscurely see,
  Through a vail that stands between.

5 Blessèd fountain, full of grace!
  Grace for sinners, grace for me;
  To this source alone I trace
  What I am, and hope to be.
  Rev. Thomas Kelly, 1809.

137 HENDON. 7. Rev. CÆSAR HENRI ABRAHAM MALAN, 1828.

1. Ask ye what great thing I know That delights and stirs me so? What the high reward I win? Whose the name I glory in? Jesus Christ, the Crucified.

2 What is faith's foundation strong?
  What awakes my lips to song?
  He who bore my sinful load,
  Purchased for me peace with God,
  Jesus Christ, the Crucified.

3 Who is Life in life to me?
  Who the Death of death will be?
  Who will place me on His right
  With the countless hosts of light?
  Jesus Christ, the Crucified.

4 This is that great thing I know;
  This delights and stirs me so:
  Faith in Him who died to save,
  Him who triumphed o'er the grave,
  Jesus Christ, the Crucified.
  Rev. Johann Cristoph Schwedler, 1711.
  Tr. by Rev. Benjamin Hall Kennedy, 1863. Ab.

NEVER ALONE.

138 LORELEI. FRIEDRICH SILCHER.

1. Far out on the des-o-late bil-low The sail-or sails the sea,
A-lone with the night and the tem-pest, Where count-less dan-gers be;

Refrain.
Yet nev-er a-lone is the Chris-tian Who lives by faith and prayer;......
4th v.—That nev-er a-lone, etc.
For God is a friend un-fail-ing, And God is ev-'ry-where.

2 Far down in the earth's dark bosom
   The miner mines the ore;
Death lurks in the dark behind him,
   And hides in the rock before;

3 Forth into the dreadful battle
   The steadfast soldier goes,
No friend, when he lies a-dying,
   His eyes to kiss and close;

4 Lord, grant, as we sail life's ocean,
   Or delve in its mines of woe,
Or fight in the terrible conflict,
   This comfort all to know:

Rossiter Worthington Raymond, 1870.

FAITHFUL FOREVER.

139 PORTUGUESE HYMN. 11.   MARC ANTOINE PORTOGALLO, 1770.

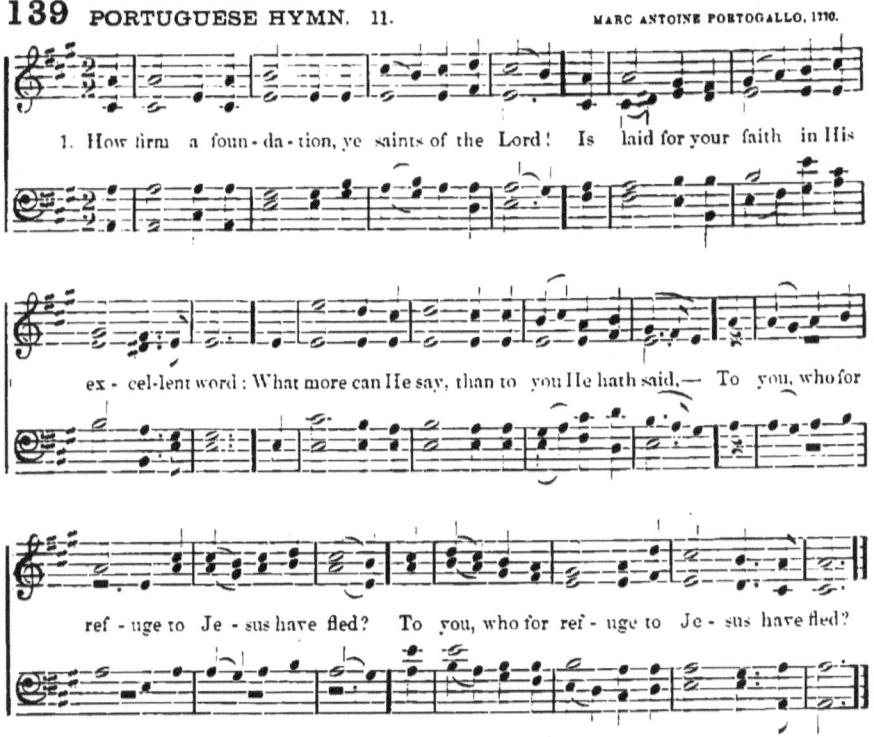

1. How firm a foun-da-tion, ye saints of the Lord! Is laid for your faith in His ex-cel-lent word: What more can He say, than to you He hath said,— To you, who for ref - uge to Je - sus have fled? To you, who for ref - uge to Je - sus have fled?

2 "Fear not, I am with thee, oh, be not dismayed,
I, I am thy God, I will still give thee aid;
I'll strengthen thee, help thee, and cause thee to stand,
Upheld by My righteous, omnipotent hand.

3 "When through the deep waters I call thee to go,
The rivers of woe shall not thee overflow;
For I will be with thee thy troubles to bless,
And sanctify to thee thy deepest distress.

4 "When through fiery trials thy pathway shall lie,
My grace, all-sufficient, shall be thy supply;
The flame shall not hurt thee; I only design
Thy dross to consume, and thy gold to refine.

5 "Ev'n down to old age all my people shall prove
My sovereign, eternal, unchangeable love;
And then, when gray hairs shall their temples adorn,
Like lambs they shall still in my bosom be borne.

6 "The soul that on Jesus hath leaned for repose,
I will not, I will not desert to his foes;
That soul, though all hell should endeavor to shake,
I'll never, no, never, no, never forsake!"

Keen, 1787. Ab.

COMFORT OF LOVE.

140 ER SORGET. 7.7.4.7.7.4.
Rev. JAMES CARTER, 1894.

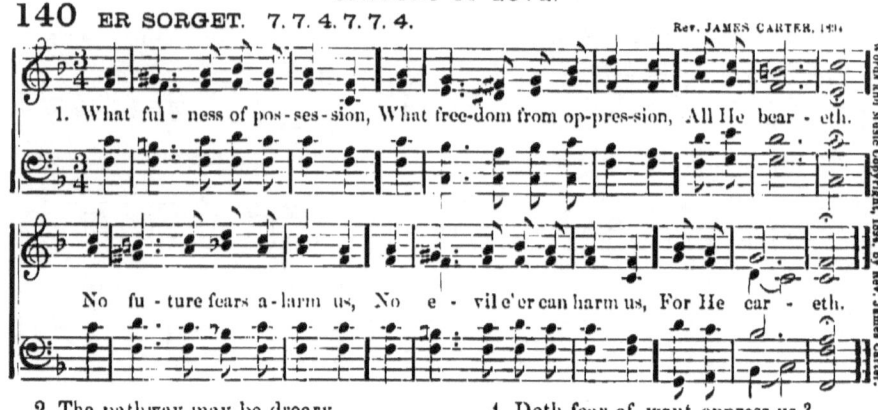

1. What ful-ness of pos-ses-sion, What free-dom from op-pres-sion, All He bear - eth.
No fu-ture fears a-larm us, No e - vil e'er can harm us, For He car - eth.

2 The pathway may be dreary,
Our feet be worn and weary,
But He shareth
Our toil; and, close beside us,
With power to guard and guide us,
Still He careth.

3 Full strong is our Defender,
Yet not more strong than tender;
And He weareth
A gentle smile for winning;
Though hearts be hard with sinning,
Still He careth.

4 Doth fear of want oppress us?
Doth dread of death distress us?
He declareth:
'Tis safe on Him relying;
For living and for dying,
Still He careth.

5 To-day He soothes our sorrow;
Bright mansions for to-morrow
He prepareth.
For all our earthly story,
For all our future glory,
Safe He careth.

Emma Smuller Carter, 1894.

141 AMICUS. 5.4. D.
Rev. JAMES CARTER, 1894.

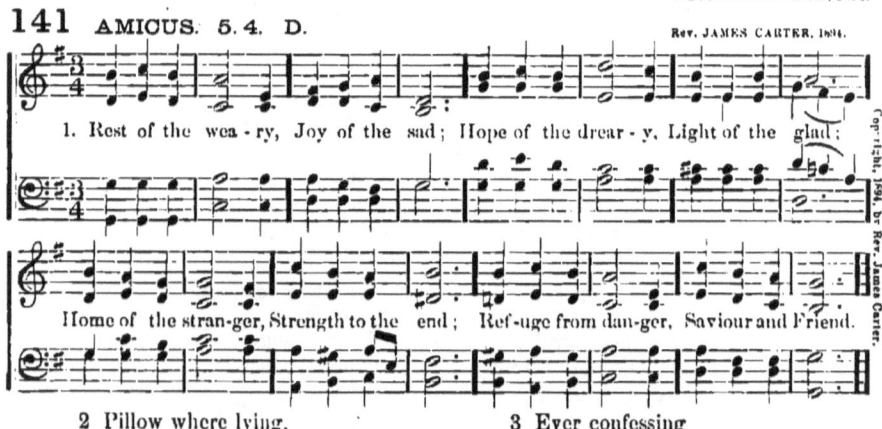

1. Rest of the wea - ry, Joy of the sad; Hope of the drear - y, Light of the glad;
Home of the stran-ger, Strength to the end; Ref-uge from dan-ger, Saviour and Friend.

2 Pillow where lying,
   Love rests its head;
Peace of the dying,
   Life of the dead;
Path of the lowly,
   Prize at the end,
Breath of the holy,
   Saviour and Friend.

3 Ever confessing
   Thee, I will raise
Unto Thee blessing,
   Glory, and praise;
All my endeavor,
   World without end,
Thine to be ever,
   Saviour and Friend!

Rev. John Samuel Bewley Monsell, 1863.

THE GOOD SHEPHERD.

142 EVAN. C. M. Rev. WILLIAM HENRY HAVERGAL, 1846. Arr. by LOWELL MASON, 1850.

1. The Lord's my Shepherd, I'll not want: He makes me down to lie
In pastures green; He leadeth me The quiet waters by.

2 My soul He doth restore again;
 And me to walk doth make
 Within the paths of righteousness,
 Ev'n for His own Name's sake.

3 Yea, though I walk in death's dark vale,
 Yet will I fear no ill;
 For Thou art with me, and Thy rod
 And staff me comfort still.

4 My table Thou hast furnished
 In presence of my foes;
 My head Thou dost with oil anoint,
 And my cup overflows.

5 Goodness and mercy, all my life,
 Shall surely follow me;
 And in God's house forevermore
 My dwelling-place shall be.
  Francis Rous, 1643. Much alt.

143 THATCHER. S. M. GEORGE FREDERICK HANDEL, 1732.

1. Behold what wondrous grace The Father has bestowed
On sinners of a mortal race, To call them sons of God!

2 Nor doth it yet appear
 How great we must be made;
 But when we see our Saviour here,
 We shall be like our Head.

3 A hope so much divine
 May trials well endure,
 May purge our souls from sense and sin,
 As Christ the Lord is pure.

4 If in my Father's love
 I share a filial part,
 Send down Thy Spirit, like a dove,
 To rest upon my heart.

5 We would no longer lie
 Like slaves beneath the throne;
 Our faith shall Abba, Father! cry,
 And Thou the kindred own.
  Rev. Isaac Watts, 1707. Ab.

THE CHRIST-FILLED LIFE.

144 LAMBETH. C. M. SAMUEL WEBBE (?) clr. 1800.

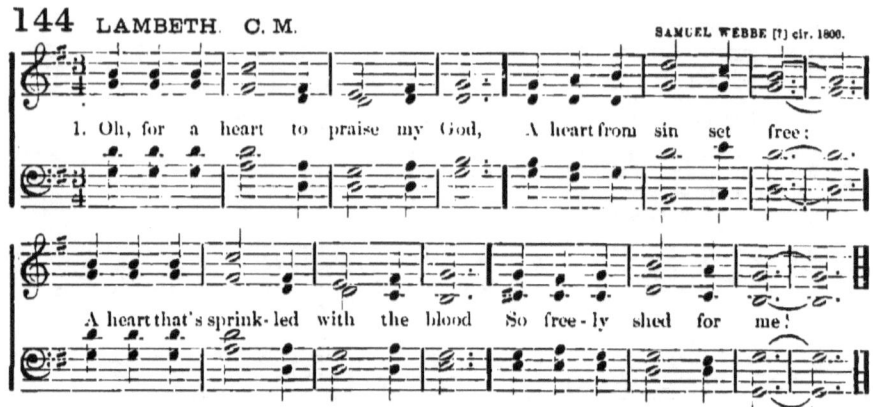

1. Oh, for a heart to praise my God, A heart from sin set free: A heart that's sprink-led with the blood So free-ly shed for me!

2 A heart resigned, submissive, meek,
  My dear Redeemer's throne;
  Where only Christ is heard to speak,
  Where Jesus reigns alone!

3 Oh, for a lowly, contrite heart,
  Believing, true, and clean;
  Which neither life nor death can part
  From Him that dwells within.

4 A heart in every thought renewed,
  And filled with love divine;
  Perfect, and right, and pure, and good;
  A copy, Lord! of Thine.

5 Thy nature, gracious Lord! impart;
  Come quickly from above;
  Write Thy new Name upon my heart,—
  Thy new, best Name of Love.
    Rev. Charles Wesley, 1742. Ab. and sl. alt.

145

1 Oh, for a closer walk with God,
  A calm and heavenly frame,—
  A light to shine upon the road
  That leads me to the Lamb!

2 Return, O holy Dove, return,
  Sweet Messenger of rest!
  I hate the sins that made Thee mourn,
  And drove Thee from my breast.

3 The dearest idol I have known,
  Whate'er that idol be,
  Help me to tear it from Thy throne,
  And worship only Thee.

4 So shall my walk be close with God,
  Calm and serene my frame;
  So purer light shall mark the road
  That leads me to the Lamb.
    William Cowper, 1772. Ab.

146

1 When I can read my title clear
  To mansions in the skies,
  I bid farewell to every fear,
  And wipe my weeping eyes.

2 Should earth against my soul engage,
  And fiery darts be hurled,
  Then I can smile at Satan's rage,
  And face a frowning world.

3 Let cares like a wild deluge come,
  And storms of sorrow fall;
  May I but safely reach my home,
  My God, my Heaven, my all!—

4 There shall I bathe my weary soul
  In seas of heavenly rest;
  And not a wave of trouble roll
  Across my peaceful breast.
    Rev. Isaac Watts, 1707.

ARLINGTON. C. M. THOMAS AUGUSTINE ARNE, 1844.

GLORYING IN THE CROSS.

147 RATHBUN. 8. 7. ITHAMAR CONKEY, 1851

1. In the cross of Christ I glory, Tow'r-ing o'er the wrecks of time;
All the light of sa - cred sto - ry Gath-ers round its head sub-lime.

2 When the woes of life o'ertake me,
  Hopes deceive, and fears annoy,
  Never shall the cross forsake me:
  Lo! it glows with peace and joy.

3 When the sun of bliss is beaming
  Light and love upon my way,
  From the cross the radiance streaming,
  Adds more luster to the day.

4 Bane and blessing, pain and pleasure,
  By the cross are sanctified;
  Peace is there, that knows no measure,
  Joys that through all time abide.

5 In the cross of Christ I glory,
  Towering o'er the wrecks of time;
  All the light of sacred story
  Gathers round its head sublime.
  Sir John Bowring, 1825.

148 ST. AGNES. C. M. Rev. JOHN BACCHUS DYKES, 1858.

1. Je - sus, these eyes have nev - er seen That ra - diant form of Thine!
The vail of sense hangs dark be - tween Thy bless - ed face and mine!

2 I see Thee not, I hear Thee not,
  Yet art Thou oft with me;
  And earth hath ne'er so dear a spot,
  As where I meet with Thee.

3 Like some bright dream that comes un-
  When slumbers o'er me roll, [sought,
  Thine image ever fills my thought,
  And charms my ravished soul.

4 Yet though I have not seen, and still
  Must rest in faith alone;
  I love Thee, dearest Lord!—and will,
  Unseen, but not unknown.

5 When death these mortal eyes shall seal,
  And still this throbbing heart,
  The rending vail shall Thee reveal,
  All glorious as Thou art!
  Rev. Ray Palmer, 1858.

CLINGING TO CHRIST.

149 FLEMMING. 8.8.8.6.
FRIEDRICH FERDINAND FLEMMING, 1810.

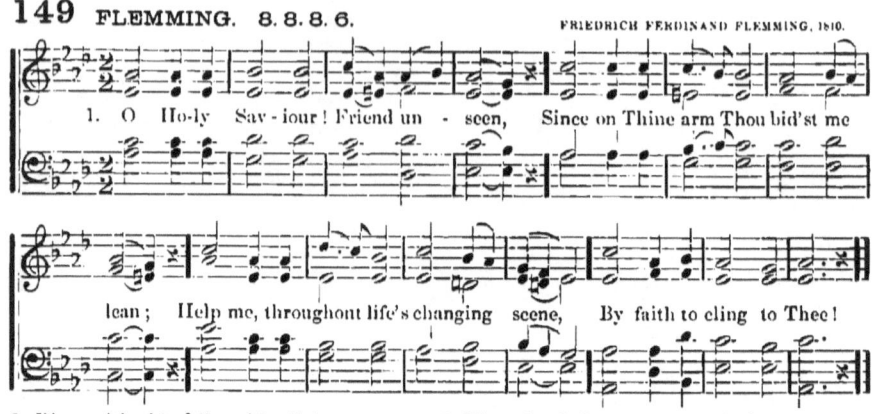

1. O Holy Saviour! Friend unseen, Since on Thine arm Thou bid'st me lean; Help me, throughout life's changing scene, By faith to cling to Thee!

2 Blest with this fellowship divine,
Take what Thou wilt, I'll not repine;
For, as the branches to the vine,
My soul would cling to Thee.

3 What though the world deceitful prove,
And earthly friends and hopes remove;
With patient uncomplaining love
Still would I cling to Thee.

4 Though oft I seem to tread alone
Life's dreary waste, with thorns o'ergrown,
Thy voice of love, in gentlest tone,
Still whispers, "Cling to Me!"

5 Though faith and hope are often tried,
I ask not, need not, aught beside;
So safe, so calm, so satisfied,
The soul that clings to Thee!

Miss Charlotte Elliott, 1834. Ab. and sl. alt.

JEWETT. 6. D.
CARL MARIA VON WEBER, 1820.
Arr. by JOSEPH PERRY HOLBROOK, 1862.

1. My Jesus, as Thou wilt! Oh! may Thy will be mine; Into Thy hand of love I would my all resign; Through sorrow or thro' joy, Conduct me as Thine own, And help me still to say, My Lord, Thy will be done!

Used by permission.

AS THOU WILT.

150 ST. ANN'S. C. M.
WILLIAM CROFT, 1708.

1. God moves in a mys-ter-ious way His won-ders to per-form; He plants His foot-steps in the sea, And rides up-on the storm.

2 Deep in unfathomable mines
Of never-failing skill,
He treasures up His bright designs,
And works His sovereign will.

3 Ye fearful saints, fresh courage take!
The clouds ye so much dread,
Are big with mercy, and will break
In blessings on your head.

4 Judge not the Lord by feeble sense,
But trust Him for His grace;
Behind a frowning providence
He hides a smiling face.

5 Blind unbelief is sure to err,
And scan His work in vain;
God is His own interpreter,
And He will make it plain.

William Cowper, 1773. Ab.

151 (JEWETT). 6. D.

1 My Jesus, as Thou wilt!
Oh! may Thy will be mine;
Into Thy hand of love
I would my all resign;
Through sorrow, or through joy,
Conduct me as Thine own,
And help me still to say,
My Lord, Thy will be done!

2 My Jesus, as Thou wilt!
Though seen through many a tear,
Let not my star of hope
Grow dim or disappear:
Since Thou on earth hast wept,
And sorrowed oft alone,
If I must weep with Thee,
My Lord, Thy will be done!

3 My Jesus, as Thou wilt!
All shall be well for me;
Each changing future scene
I gladly trust with Thee:
Straight to my home above
I travel calmly on,
And sing, in life or death,
My Lord, Thy will be done!

Rev. Benjamin Schmolke, 1716.
Tr. by Miss Jane Borthwick, 1854. Ab.

152 6. D.

1 Thy way, not mine, O Lord,
However dark it be!
Lead me by Thine own hand;
Choose out the path for me.
I dare not choose my lot:
I would not, if I might;
Choose Thou for me, my God,
So shall I walk aright.

2 The kingdom that I seek,
Is Thine; so let the way
That leads to it be Thine,
Else I must surely stray.
Take Thou my cup, and it
With joy or sorrow fill,
As best to Thee may seem;
Choose Thou my good and ill.

3 Choose Thou for me my friends,
My sickness or my health;
Choose Thou my cares for me,
My poverty or wealth.
Not mine, not mine the choice,
In things or great or small;
Be Thou my Guide, my Strength,
My Wisdom, and my All.

Rev. Horatius Bonar, 1857. Ab.

THE PEACE OF GOD.

153 CALVARY. C.M.
LUDWIG SPOHR, 1835.
Arr. by C. ARTHUR JACQUES, 1895.

1. O Thou, whose bounty fills my cup With ev-'ry bless-ing meet! I give Thee thanks for ev-'ry drop— The bit-ter and the sweet.

2 I praise Thee for the desert road,
 And for the river-side;
For all Thy goodness hath bestowed,
 And all Thy grace denied.
3 I thank Thee for both smile and frown,
 And for the gain and loss;
I praise Thee for the future crown,
 And for the present cross.
4 I thank Thee for the wing of love,
 Which stirred my worldly nest;
And for the stormy clouds which drove
 The flutterer to Thy breast.
5 I bless Thee for the glad increase,
 And for the waning joy;
And for this strange, this settled peace,
 Which nothing can destroy.
Jane Crewdson, 1860.

154
1 We bless Thee for Thy peace, O God!
 Deep as the soundless sea,
Which falls like sunshine on the road
 Of those who trust in Thee.
2 That peace which suffers and is strong,
 Trusts where it cannot see,
Deems not the trial way too long,
 But leaves the end with Thee;—
3 That peace which flows serene and deep—
 A river in the soul,
Whose banks a living verdure keep:
 God's sunshine o'er the whole!
4 Such, Father, give our hearts such peace,
 Whate'er the outward be,
Till all life's discipline shall cease,
 And we go home to Thee.
Unknown Writer, 1858. Ab.

155 (RUBINSTEIN). 7.
1 In the dark and cloudy day,
 When earth's riches flee away,
 And the last hope will not stay,
  Saviour, comfort me!
2 When the secret idol's gone
 That my poor heart yearned upon,—
 Desolate, bereft, alone,
  Saviour, comfort me!
3 Thou, who wast so sorely tried,
 In the darkness crucified,
 Bid me in Thy love confide;
  Saviour, comfort me!
4 So it shall be good for me
 Much afflicted now to be,
 If Thou wilt but tenderly,
  Saviour, comfort me!
George Rawson, 1853. Ab.

156 7.
1 Holy Ghost, the Infinite!
 Shine upon our nature's night
 With Thy blessed inward light,
  Comforter Divine!
2 We are sinful: cleanse us, Lord;
 We are faint: Thy strength afford;
 Lost,—until by Thee restored,
  Comforter Divine!
3 Like the dew, Thy peace distill;
 Guide, subdue our wayward will,
 Things of Christ unfolding still,
  Comforter Divine!
4 Search for us the depths of God;
 Bear us up the starry road,
 To the hight of Thine abode,
  Comforter Divine!
George Rawson, 1853. Ab. and st. alt.

157 DEDICATION. 8.7.8.8.8.7.
Rev. JAMES CARTER, 1895.

1. Jesus, Saviour, Thou hast sought me
Wandering and lost and lone;
With Thy precious blood hast bought me,
To Thy shelt'ring fold hast brought me,
Tenderly hast trained and taught me,
May I follow Thee alone.

2 When the world, my heart alluring,
   Softly calls, in tempting tone;
   Then the right resolve insuring,
   And my faltering step securing,
   Make me faithful and enduring;
   May I follow Thee alone.

3 Since from bondage Thou hast freed me,
   I no future bondage own,
   But the bonds of love, that lead me
   Through green fields where Thou dost feed me,
   All the way Thou hast decreed me,
   Smooth or thorny, to Thy throne.

Emma Smuller Carter, 1895.

RUBINSTEIN. 7.
ANTON GREGOR RUBINSTEIN,
Arr. by C. ARTHUR JACQUES, 1899.

1. In the dark and cloudy day,
When earth's riches flee away,
And the last hope will not stay,
Saviour, comfort me!

CLOSER TO THEE.

158 ROBINSON. 6. 4. 6. 4. 6. 6. 6. 4.   Rev. JAMES CARTER, 1876.

1. Saviour! I follow on, Guided by Thee, Seeing not yet the hand That leadeth me; Hushed be my heart and still, Fear I no further ill, Only to meet Thy will My will shall be.

2 Riven the rock for me
  Thirst to relieve,
Manna from Heaven falls
  Fresh every eve;
Never a want severe
Causeth my eye a tear,
But Thou dost whisper near,
  "Only believe!"

3 Often to Marah's brink
  Have I been brought;
Shrinking the cup to drink,
  Help I have sought;
And with the prayer's ascent,
Jesus the branch hath rent,
Quickly relief hath sent,
  Sweetening the draught.

4 Saviour! I long to walk
  Closer with Thee;
Led by Thy guiding hand,
  Ever to be;
Constantly near Thy side,
Quickened and purified,
Living for Him who died
  Freely for me!
        Rev. Charles Seymour Robinson, 1862.

159

1 I'm but a stranger here,
  Heaven is my home;
Earth is a desert drear,
  Heaven is my home;
Danger and sorrow stand
Round me on every hand;
Heaven is my fatherland;
  Heaven is my home.

2 What though the tempest rage,
  Heaven is my home;
Short is my pilgrimage,
  Heaven is my home;
Time's wild and wintry blast
Soon will be overpast;
I shall reach home at last,
  Heaven is my home.

3 There at my Saviour's side—
  Heaven is my home—
I shall be glorified,
  Heaven is my home;
There are the good and blest,
Those I loved most and best,
And there I too shall rest;
  Heaven is my home.
      Rev. Thomas Rawson Taylor, 1836. Ab.

PRAYER FOR GUIDANCE.

160 WALTER. 7. 3. 7. 7. 7. 3.

EMMA SMULLER CARTER, 1894.
Arr. by Rev. JAMES CARTER, 1894.

1. Je-sus, Sav-iour, be my guide, All the way, Tho' the clouds Thy face may hide, Con-stant still Thou dost a-bide; I shall all the storms out-ride Some sweet day.

2 Jesus, Saviour, be my guide,
  All the way.
Naught of harm can e'er betide,
Naught of good shall be denied;
But I shall be satisfied
  Some sweet day.

3 Jesus, Saviour, be my guide,
  All the way.
All to Thee I would confide;
Lead me, lead me to Thy side;
There may I be glorified
  Some sweet day.

Emma Smuller Carter, 1894.

161 DIX. 7. 6 l.

CONRAD KOCHER, 1838.
WILLIAM HENRY MONK, 1861.

1. { Lord, Thy chil-dren guide and keep, As with fee-ble steps they press
     On the path-way rough and steep, Thro' this wea-ry wil-der-ness: }
   Ho-ly Je-sus! day by day Lead us in the nar-row way.

2 There are sandy wastes that lie
    Cold and sunless, vast and drear,
  Where the feeble faint and die,
    Grant us grace to persevere:
  Holy Jesus! day by day
  Lead us in the narrow way.

3 There are soft and flowery glades,
    Decked with golden-fruited trees,—
  Sunny slopes, and scented shades;

  Keep us, Lord, from slothful ease:
  Holy Jesus! day by day
  Lead us in the narrow way.

4 Upward still to purer hights,
    Onward yet to scenes more blest,
  Calmer regions, clearer lights,
    Till we reach the promised rest!
  Holy Jesus! day by day
  Lead us in the narrow way.

Bp. William Walsham How, 1854.

THE LEADING LIGHT.

162 LUX BENIGNA. 10. 4. 10. 10.   Rev. JOHN BACCHUS DYKES, 1861.

1. Lead, kindly Light, a-mid th' encircling gloom, Lead Thou me on; The night is dark, and I am far from home, Lead Thou me on; Keep Thou my feet; I do not ask to see The dis-tant scene, one step e-nough for me.

2 I was not ever thus, nor prayed that Thou
    Shouldst lead me on;
  I loved to choose and see my path; but now
    Lead Thou me on!
  I loved the garish day, and, spite of fears,
  Pride ruled my will. Remember not
    past years!

3 So long Thy power has blest me, sure it still
    Will lead me on
  O'er moor and fen, o'er crag and torrent, till
    The night is gone,
  And with the morn those angel faces smile
  Which I have loved long since, and lost
    awhile!

                                    Rev. John Henry Newman, 1833.

LIVORNO. 7.   PIETRO MASCAGNI, 1890.
                               Arr. by C. ARTHUR JACQUES, 1897.

1. Mine to fol-low, Thine to lead, This through all the Word I read, This thro' all my life I learn, Taught a-new at ev-'ry turn.

Words and Music Copyright, 1899, by Emma Smauler Carter.

THE LORD OUR LEADER.

163 GERTRUDE. 6. 5. 12 1. Sir. ARTHUR SEYMOUR SULLIVAN, 1872.

1. Onward, Christian soldiers, Marching as to war, With the cross of Jesus Going on before. Christ, the royal Master, Leads against the foe; Forward into battle, See His banner go. Onward, Christian soldiers, Marching as to war, With the cross of Jesus, Going on before.

2 Like a mighty army
  Moves the Church of God,
  Brothers, we are treading
  Where the saints have trod;
  We are not divided,
  All one body we,
  One in hope and doctrine,
  One in charity.

3 Crowns and thrones may perish,
  Kingdoms rise and wane,
  But the Church of Jesus,
  Constant will remain.
  Gates of hell can never
  'Gainst that Church prevail,
  We have Christ's own promise,
  And that cannot fail.

4 Onward, then, ye people,
  Join our happy throng,
  Blend with ours your voices
  In the triumph song;
  Glory, laud and honor
  Unto Christ the King,
  This through countless ages,
  Men and angels sing.
      Rev. Sabine Baring-Gould, 1865.

---

164 (LIVORNO). 7.

1 Mine to follow, Thine to lead,
  This through all the Word I read;
  This through all my life I learn,
  Taught anew at every turn.

2 Every effort made to bless,
  Every failure or success,
  Every path in darkness trod,
  Guided by the hand of God.

3 Every step I take amiss,
  Every triumph, teaches this;
  This the law by love decreed:
  Mine to follow, Thine to lead.
      Emma Smuller Carter, 1897.

THE GOOD SHEPHERD.

165 HODNET. 7. 6. D.   SIGISMUND THALBERG. 1850.

1. { In heav'n-ly love a-bid-ing, No change my heart shall fear, }
   { And safe is such con-fid-ing, [Omit................] }
   For noth-ing chang-es here: The storm may roar with-out me,
   My heart may low be laid, But God is round a-bout me, And can I be dismayed?

2 Wherever He may guide me,
   No want shall turn me back ;
  My Shepherd is beside me,
   And nothing can I lack :
  His wisdom ever waketh,
   His sight is never dim :
  He knows the way He taketh,
   And I will walk with Him.

3 Green pastures are before me,
   Which yet I have not seen :
  Bright skies will soon be o'er me,
   Where darkest clouds have been :
  My hope I cannot measure,
   My path to life is free ;
  My Saviour has my treasure,
   And He will walk with me.
     Miss Anna Laetitia Waring, 1850. St. alt.

BERLIN. 7.   GEORG CHRISTOPH STRATTNER 1691.
Rev. JOHANN ANASTASIUS FREYLINGHAUSEN. 1705.

1. Sav-iour, teach me, day by day, Love's sweet les-son, — to o-bey;
Sweet-er les-son can-not be, Lov-ing Him who first loved me.

THE PILLAR OF FIRE.

166 REGENT SQUARE. 8.7.4.   HENRY SMART, 1867.

1. Guide me, O Thou great Jehovah, Pilgrim through this barren land; I am weak, but Thou art mighty; Hold me with Thy pow'rful hand; Bread of Heaven, Bread of Heaven, Feed me till I want no more.

2 Open Thou the crystal fountain
  Whence the healing streams do flow;
  Let the fiery, cloudy pillar
    Lead me all my journey through;
      Strong Deliverer,
  Be Thou still my Strength and Shield.

3 When I tread the verge of Jordan,
  Bid my anxious fears subside;
  Death of death! and hell's Destruction!
    Land me safe on Canaan's side;
      Songs of praises
  I will ever give to Thee.
Rev. William Williams, 1745, 1772. Ab.
Rev. Peter Williams, tr. v. 1, 1771.

167

1 Lead us, heavenly Father, lead us
  O'er the world's tempestuous sea;
  Guard us, guide us, keep us, feed us,
    For we have no help but Thee;
      Yet possessing Every blessing,
  If our God our Father be.

2 Saviour, breathe forgiveness o'er us;
  All our weakness Thou dost know;
  Thou didst tread this earth before us;
    Thou didst feel its keenest woe;
      Lone and dreary, Faint and weary,
  Through the desert Thou didst go.

3 Spirit of our God, descending,
  Fill our hearts with heavenly joy;
  Love with every passion blending,
    Pleasure that can never cloy;
      Thus provided, Pardoned, guided,
  Nothing can our peace destroy.
James Edmeston, 1821.

168 (BERLIN). 7.

1 Saviour! teach me, day by day,
  Love's sweet lesson,—to obey;
  Sweeter lesson cannot be,
  Loving Him who first loved me.

2 With a child-like heart of love,
  At Thy bidding may I move;
  Prompt to serve and follow Thee,
  Loving Him who first loved me.

3 Teach me all Thy steps to trace,
  Strong to follow in Thy grace;
  Learning how to love from Thee,
  Loving Him who first loved me.

4 Thus may I rejoice to show
  That I feel the love I owe;
  Singing, till Thy face I see,
  Of His love who first loved me.
Miss Jane E. Leeson, 1842. Ab.

THE WIND CEASED.

...ev-er it be, No wa-ters can swal-low the ship where lies The Mas-ter of o-cean, and earth, and skies; They all shall sweet-ly o-bey Thy will, Peace, be still! Peace, be still! They all shall sweet-ly o-bey Thy will, Peace, peace, be still!

2 Master, with anguish of spirit
  I bow in my grief to-day;
The depths of my sad heart are troubled—
  Oh, waken and save, I pray!
Torrents of sin and of anguish
  Sweep o'er my sinking soul;
And I perish! I perish! dear Master—
  Oh, hasten, and take control!

3 Master, the terror is over,
  The elements sweetly rest;
Earth's sun in the calm lake is mirrored,
  And Heaven's within my breast;
Linger, O blessèd Redeemer!
  Leave me alone no more;
And with joy I shall make the blest harbor,
  And rest on the blissful shore.

Miss Mary A. Baker, 1874.

170   BARTIMEUS.   8. 7.

STEPHEN JENKS, 1805.

1. "Je-sus on-ly!" In the shad-ow Of the cloud so chill and dim,
2. "Je-sus on-ly!" In the glo-ry, When the shad-ows all are flown,

We are cling-ing, lov-ing, trust-ing, He with us, and we with Him.
See-ing Him in all His beau-ty, Sat-is-fied with Him a-lone.

Frances Ridley Havergal, 1870.   Ab.

THE DIVINE PILOT.

171 PILOT. 7. 6 l.   JOHN EDGAR GOULD, 1871.

1. Jesus, Saviour, pilot me, O-ver life's tempestuous sea;
D.C.—Chart and compass came from Thee: Jesus, Saviour, pilot me.

Un-known waves before me roll, Hiding rock and treacherous shoal;

2 As a mother stills her child,
  Thou canst hush the ocean wild;
  Boisterous waves obey Thy will
  When Thou say'st to them "Be still!"
  Wondrous Sovereign of the sea,
  Jesus, Saviour, pilot me.

3 When at last I near the shore,
  And the fearful breakers roar
  'Twixt me and the peaceful rest,
  Then, while leaning on Thy breast,
  May I hear Thee say to me,
  "Fear not, I will pilot thee!"
                    Rev. Edward Hopper, 1871.

172 HENDON. 7.   Rev. HENRI ABRAHAM CÆSAR MALAN, 1827.

1. Children of the heav'nly King, As ye journey, sweetly sing! Sing your Saviour's worthy praise, Glorious in His works and ways! Glorious in His works and ways!

2 Ye are traveling home to God
  In the way the fathers trod;
  They are happy now, and ye
  Soon their happiness shall see.

3 Shout, ye little flock, and blest!
  You on Jesus' throne shall rest;
  There your seat is now prepared;
  There your kingdom and reward.

4 Lord, submissive make us go,
  Gladly leaving all below;
  Only Thou our leader be,
  And we still will follow Thee.
                    Rev. John Cennick, 1742. Ab.

GUIDANCE.

173 LEAD ME, SAVIOUR. 7. With Refrain. FRANK M. DAVIS, 1882.

2 Thou the refuge of my soul
When life's stormy billows roll,
I am safe when Thou art nigh,
All my hopes on Thee rely.

3 Saviour, lead me, then at last,
When the storm of life is past,
To the land of endless day,
Where all tears are wiped away.
                    Frank M. Davis, 1882.

GOOD CHEER.

174 BON CŒUR. C. M. D. Rev. JAMES CARTER, 1896.

1. A-long the high-way of the King My pil-grim steps I tread,
His streams of liv-ing grace I sing, By food ce-les-tial fed;
All night, a-bove the gloom-y hights, His guid-ing stars shine clear;
All day His sun my path de-lights, While love casts out all fear.

Words and Music Copyright, 1899, by Rev. James Carter.

2 Through fields of green I follow on,
   By waters deep and still,
Through darkling clefts where He has [gone,
   Secure from every ill;
And, though the angry clouds appall,
   The night be drear and cold,
I yet can hear His loving call,
   And reach the sheltering fold.

3 When, pierced by Satan's venomed dart,
   Beside the way I fall;
His love revives my fainting heart,
   And bears me safe through all;
And so I journey in His might,
   Though pressed by grief and care,
While He makes every burden light
   Or gives me strength to bear.

4 Exulting in His gracious care,
   My pilgrim staff I take,
Ascending to the mountains fair
   Where bars of dawning break;
There Zion's golden ramparts bright
   In crimson glow I see,
And on His throne the Lord of light
   Awaits to welcome me.

Rev. James Carter, 1897.

THE HOLY WAR.

175 ALL SAINTS. C. M. D. HENRY STEPHEN CUTLER, 1872.

1. The Son of God goes forth to war, A kingly crown to gain;
His blood-red banner streams afar; Who follows in His train?
Who best can drink his cup of woe, Triumphant over pain;
Who patient bears his cross below, He follows in His train.

2 The martyr first, whose eagle eye
  Could pierce beyond the grave,
Who saw his Master in the sky,
  And called on Him to save:
Like Him, with pardon on his tongue,
  In midst of mortal pain,
He prayed for them that did the wrong:
  Who follows in his train?

3 A glorious band, the chosen few,
  On whom the Spirit came :
Twelve valiant saints, their hope they knew,
  And mocked the cross and flame:
They met the tyrant's brandished steel,
  The lion's gory mane ;
They bowed their necks the death to feel :
  Who follows in their train?

4 A noble army, men and boys,
  The matron and the maid,
Around the Saviour's throne rejoice,
  In robes of light arrayed :
They climbed the steep ascent of Heaven
  Through peril, toil, and pain :
O God, to us may grace be given
  To follow in their train.

        Bp. Reginald Heber, 1827.

THE GOOD FIGHT.

176 PARK STREET. L. M. FREDERIC MARC ANTOINE VENUA, 1810.

1. Stand up, my soul, shake off thy fears, And gird the gos-pel arm-or on; March to the gates of endless joy, Where Jesus, thy great Captain's gone, Where Jesus, thy great Captain's gone.

177

2 Hell and thy sins resist thy course;
   But hell and sin are vanquished foes;
   Thy Saviour nailed them to the cross,
   And sung the triumph when He rose.

3 Then let my soul march boldly on,—
   Press forward to the heavenly gate;
   There peace and joy eternal reign, [wait.
   And glittering robes for conquerors

4 There shall I wear a starry crown,
   And triumph in almighty grace,
   While all the armies of the skies
   Join in my glorious Leader's praise.
         Rev. Isaac Watts, 1707. Ab. and sl. alt.

1 Fight the good fight with all thy might,
   Christ is thy strength, and Christ thy right;
   Lay hold on life, and it shall be
   Thy joy and crown eternally.

2 Run the straight race thro' God's good
   Lift up thine eyes, and seek His face; [grace,
   Life with its way before us lies,
   Christ is the path, and Christ the prize.

3 Faint not, nor fear, His arms are near,
   He changeth not, and thou art dear;
   Only believe, and thou shalt see
   That Christ is All in all to thee.
         Rev. John Samuel Bewley Monsell, 1863. Ab.

178 DUKE STREET. L. M. JOHN HATTON, c. 1790.

1. 'Tis by the faith of joys to come We walk thro' des-erts dark as night; Till we ar-rive at Heaven, our home, Faith is our guide, and faith our light.

2 The want of sight she well supplies,
   She makes the pearly gates appear;
   Far into distant worlds she pries,
   And brings eternal glories near.

3 Cheerful we tread the desert through,
   While faith inspires a heavenly ray;
   Though lions roar, and tempests blow,
   And rocks and dangers fill the way.
         Rev. Isaac Watts, 1709. Ab.

VIGILANCE.

179 LABAN. S. M. LOWELL MASON, 1830.

1. My soul, be on thy guard, Ten thousand foes arise;
And hosts of sin are pressing hard To draw thee from the skies.

2 Oh, watch, and fight, and pray!
   The battle ne'er give o'er;
Renew it boldly every day,
   And help divine implore.

3 Ne'er think the victory won,
   Nor once at ease sit down;
Thy arduous work will not be done
   Till thou obtain thy crown.

4 Fight on, my soul, till death
   Shall bring thee to thy God!
He'll take thee at thy parting breath,
   Up to His blest abode.
Rev. George Heath, 1781. Sl. alt.

180

1 My soul, weigh not thy life
   Against thy heavenly crown,
Nor suffer Satan's deadliest strife
   To beat thy courage down.

2 With prayer and crying strong,
   Maintain the fearful fight,
And let the breaking day prolong
   The wrestling of the night.

3 The battle soon will yield,
   If thou thy part fulfill;
For strong as is the hostile shield,
   Thy sword is stronger still.

4 Thine armor is divine,
   Thy feet with victory shod;
And on thy head shall quickly shine
   The diadem of God.
Rev. Leonard Swain, 1858. Sl. alt.

181 BOYLSTON. S. M. LOWELL MASON, 1832.

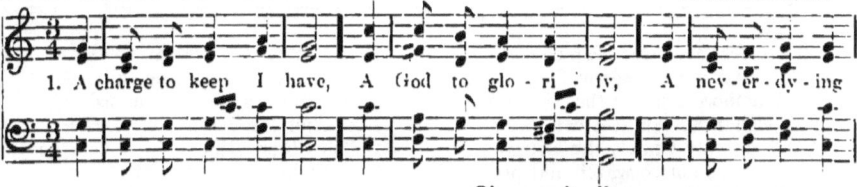

1. A charge to keep I have, A God to glorify, A never-dying
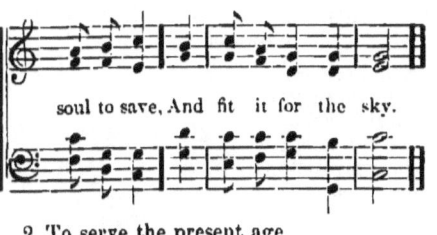
soul to save, And fit it for the sky.

2 To serve the present age,
   My calling to fulfill;
Oh, may it all my powers engage
   To do my Master's will.

3 Arm me with jealous care,
   As in Thy sight to live;
And oh, Thy servant, Lord, prepare
   A strict account to give.

4 Help me to watch and pray,
   And on Thyself rely,
Assured, if I my trust betray,
   I shall forever die.
Rev. Charles Wesley, 1762.

CONFLICT AND CONQUEST.

182. HAMNER. C. M. D. With Refrain.

Rev. JAMES CARTER. 1898.

1. Go forward, Christian soldier, Beneath His banner true: The Lord Himself, thy Leader, Shall all thy foes subdue. His love foretells thy trials, He knows thine hourly need; He can, with bread of Heaven, Thy fainting spirit feed. Go

Ref.—forward, Christian soldier, Beneath His banner true: The Lord Himself, thy Leader, Shall all thy foes subdue.

2 Go forward, Christian soldier;
  Fear not the secret foe;
Far more are o'er thee watching
  Than human eyes can know.
Trust only Christ, thy Captain,
  Cease not to watch and pray;
Heed not the treacherous voices,
  That lure thy soul astray.

3 Go forward, Christian soldier,
  Nor dream of peaceful rest,
Till Satan's host is vanquished,
  And Heaven is all possessed;
Till Christ Himself shall call thee
  To lay thine armor by,
And wear, in endless glory,
  The crown of victory.

4 Go forward, Christian soldier,
  Fear not the gathering night;
The Lord has been thy shelter,
  The Lord will be thy light;
When morn His face revealeth,
  Thy dangers all are past;
O pray that faith and virtue
  May keep thee to the last.

Rev. Lawrence Tuttiett, 1861.

OVERCOMING.

183 TEMPTATION. P. M.
HORATIO RICHMOND PALMER, 1868.

1. Yield not to tempta-tion, For yielding is sin, Each vict'ry will help you
   Fight man-ful-ly on-ward, Dark passions sub-due, Look ev-er to Je-sus,
   Some oth-er to win; }
   (Omit..................) He'll car-ry you through. Ask the Saviour to help you,
   Comfort, strengthen, and keep you; He is willing to aid you, He will car-ry you through.

2 Shun evil companions,
  Bad language disdain,
  God's Name hold in reverence,
  Nor take it in vain;
  Be thoughtful and earnest,
  Kind-hearted and true,
  Look ever to Jesus,
  He will carry you through.

3 To him that o'ercometh
  God giveth a crown,
  Through faith we shall conquer,
  Though often cast down;
  He, who is our Saviour,
  Our strength will renew,
  Look ever to Jesus,
  He will carry you through.

  Horatio Richmond Palmer, 1868.

184 VIGILATE. 7. 7. 7. 3.
WILLIAM HENRY MONK, 1874.

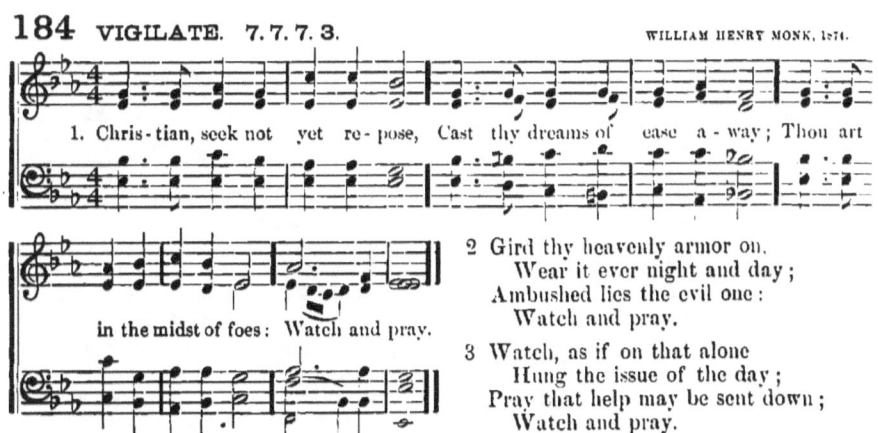

1. Chris-tian, seek not yet re-pose, Cast thy dreams of ease a-way; Thou art
   in the midst of foes: Watch and pray.

2 Gird thy heavenly armor on,
  Wear it ever night and day;
  Ambushed lies the evil one:
  Watch and pray.

3 Watch, as if on that alone
  Hung the issue of the day;
  Pray that help may be sent down;
  Watch and pray.

Miss Charlotte Elliott, 1839. Ab. and sl. alt.

185 CHRISTMAS. C. M.
GEORGE FREDERICK HANDEL, 1728.

1. Awake, my soul, stretch ev'ry nerve, And press with vigor on; A heav'nly race demands thy zeal, And an immortal crown, And an immortal crown.

2 A cloud of witnesses around
Hold thee in full survey;
Forget the steps already trod,
And onward urge thy way.

3 'Tis God's all-animating voice,
That calls thee from on high;
'Tis His own hand presents the prize
To thine aspiring eye.

4 Blest Saviour, introduced by Thee,
Have I my race begun;
And, crowned with victory, at Thy feet
I'll lay my honors down.

Rev. Philip Doddridge, 1755. Ab.

186 ARLINGTON. C. M.
THOMAS AUGUSTINE ARNE, 1744.

1. Am I a soldier of the cross, A follower of the Lamb? And shall I fear to own His cause, Or blush to speak His Name?

2 Must I be carried to the skies
On flowery beds of ease?
While others fought to win the prize,
And sailed through bloody seas?

3 Are there no foes for me to face?
Must I not stem the flood?
Is this vile world a friend to grace,
To help me on to God?

4 Sure I must fight, if I would reign;
Increase my courage, Lord!
I'll bear the toil, endure the pain,
Supported by Thy word.

5 Thy saints, in all this glorious war,
Shall conquer, though they die;
They view the triumph from afar,
And seize it with their eye.

6 When that illustrious day shall rise,
And all Thy armies shine
In robes of victory through the skies,
The glory shall be Thine.

Rev. Isaac Watts, 1723.

PILGRIMAGE.

187 RENOVATION. S. M.
JOHANN NEPOMUK HUMMEL. 1832.

1. The people of the Lord Are on their way to Heaven;
There they obtain their great reward; The prize will there be given.

2 'Tis conflict here below;
  In Heaven our conflicts cease:
On earth we wrestle with the foe;
  'Tis triumph there, and peace.

3 'Tis gloom and darkness here;
  'Tis light and joy above;
There all is pure, and all is clear;
  There all is peace and love.

4 There rest shall follow toil,
  And ease succeed to care;
The victors there divide the spoil;
  They sing and triumph there.

5 Then let us joyful sing:
  The conflict is not long:
We hope in Heaven to praise our King
  In one eternal song.

Rev. Thomas Kelly, 1820. Sl. alt.

188 MAITLAND. C. M.
GEORGE NELSON ALLEN, 1850.

1. Must Jesus bear the cross alone, And all the world go free?
No, there's a cross for ev-'ry one, And there's a cross for me.

2 This consecrated cross I'll bear,
    Till death shall set me free,
  And then go home my crown to wear,
    For there's a crown for me.

3 Upon the crystal pavement, down
    At Jesus' piercèd feet,
  Joyful, I'll cast my golden crown,
    And His dear Name repeat.

4 And palms shall wave, and harps shall ring,
    Beneath Heaven's arches high;
  The Lord that lives, the ransomed sing,
    That lives no more to die.

5 Oh, precious cross! oh, glorious crown!
    Oh, resurrection day!
  Ye angels, from the stars flash down,
    And bear my soul away.

Rev. Thomas Shepherd, 1793, v. 1 alt.
Rev. Charles Beecher, 1855, vv. 3, 5.
vv. 2 and 4 anon., 1849.

189 HOLLINGSIDE. 7. D.

Rev. JOHN BACCHUS DYKES.

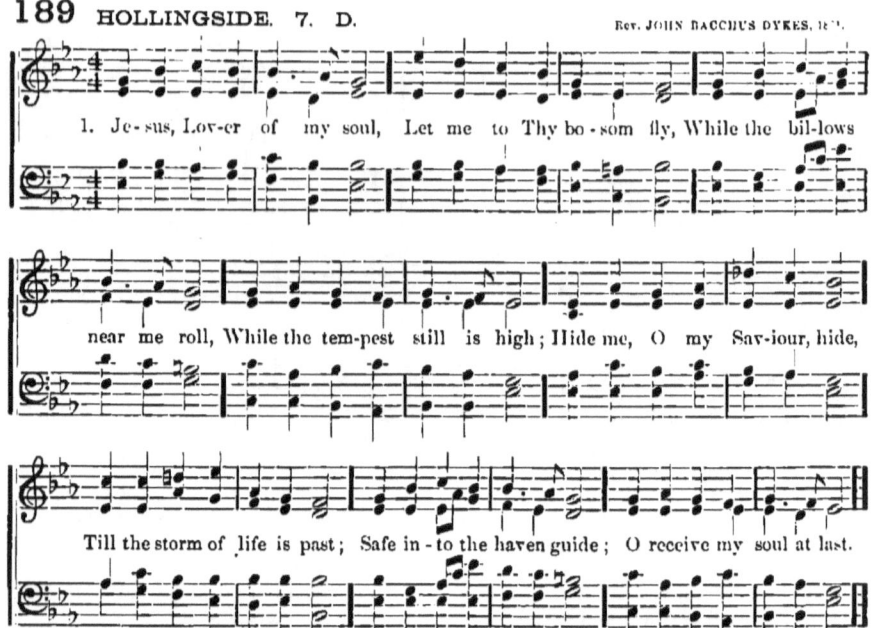

1. Jesus, Lover of my soul, Let me to Thy bosom fly, While the billows near me roll, While the tempest still is high; Hide me, O my Saviour, hide, Till the storm of life is past; Safe into the haven guide; O receive my soul at last.

2 Other refuge have I none;
    Hangs my helpless soul on Thee;
Leave, ah! leave me not alone,
    Still support and comfort me.
All my trust on Thee is stayed;
    All my help from Thee I bring;
Cover my defenceless head
    With the shadow of Thy wing.

3 Wilt Thou not regard my call?
    Wilt Thou not accept my prayer?
Lo, I sink, I faint, I fall!
    Lo, on Thee I cast my care.
Reach me out Thy gracious hand,
    While I of Thy strength receive,
Hoping against hope I stand,
    Dying, and behold I live.

4 Thou, O Christ! art all I want;
    More than all in Thee I find;
Raise the fallen, cheer the faint,
    Heal the sick, and lead the blind.
Just and holy is Thy Name,
    I am all unrighteousness;
Vile and full of sin I am,
    Thou art full of truth and grace.

5 Plenteous grace with Thee is found,—
    Grace to pardon all my sin;
Let the healing streams abound,
    Make and keep me pure within;
Thou of life the fountain art,
    Freely let me take of Thee;
Spring Thou up within my heart,
    Rise to all eternity.

Rev. Charles Wesley, 1740.

MARTYN. 7. D.

SIMEON BUTLER MARSH, 1834.

THE NOISE OF BATTLE.

190 WEBB. 7. 6. D. GEORGE JAMES WEBB, 1830.

1. Stand up!—stand up for Jesus! Ye soldiers of the cross;
Lift high His royal banner, It must not suffer loss:
From vict'ry unto vict'ry His army shall He lead,
D.S.—Till ev'ry foe is vanquished, And Christ is Lord indeed.

2 Stand up!—stand up for Jesus!
  The trumpet call obey;
Forth to the mighty conflict,
  In this His glorious day:
"Ye that are men, now serve Him,"
  Against unnumbered foes;
Let courage rise with danger,
  And strength to strength oppose.

3 Stand up!—stand up for Jesus!
  Stand in His strength alone;
The arm of flesh will fail you—
  Ye dare not trust your own:
Put on the gospel armor,
  Each piece put on with prayer,
Where duty calls, or danger,
  Be never wanting there.

4 Stand up!—stand up for Jesus!
  The strife will not be long;
This day, the noise of battle,
  The next, the victor's song;
To him that overcometh,
  A crown of life shall be;
He with the King of glory
  Shall reign eternally!
      Rev. George Duffield, 1858. Ab.

191

1 Sometimes a light surprises
  The Christian while he sings;
It is the Lord who rises
  With healing in His wings:
When comforts are declining,
  He grants the soul again
A season of clear shining,
  To cheer it after rain.

2 In holy contemplation,
  We sweetly then pursue
The theme of God's salvation,
  And find it ever new:
Set free from present sorrow,
  We cheerfully can say,
Let the unknown to-morrow
  Bring with it what it may.

3 It can bring with it nothing,
  But He will bring us through;
Who gives the lilies clothing,
  Will clothe His people too:
Beneath the spreading heavens,
  No creature but is fed;
And He who feeds the ravens,
  Will give His children bread.
      William Cowper, 1779. Ab.

ONLY A VOICE.

192 VOX CLAMANTIS.

Rev. JAMES CARTER, 1894.

1. On-ly a voice in the des-ert of sin, Pro-claim-ing, "Re-pent and be-lieve," A strong, sweet voice that may wak-en and win To the Sav-iour who waits to re-ceive. On-ly a voice with a clear, strong cry, A word to the souls that are read-y to die. List-en, my broth-er, are you, am I, Read-y to speak for the Lord?

2 Only a life to be lived in His name,
 A life of devotion and love,
Of daily deeds that shall plainly proclaim
 That our citizenship is above.
Only a life that is lived on high,
 Uplifting the souls that are ready to die.
Listen, my brother, are you, am I,
 Ready to live for the Lord?

3 Only a day for the work that our Lord
 Has left for the faithful to do.
What deeds of love do the moments record,
 O my brother, for me and for you?
Only a day that will quickly fly,
 And then an account to be given on high.
Listen, my brother, are you, am I,
 Ready to answer the Lord?

Emma Smuller Carter, 1894.

CHRISTIAN ACTIVITY.

193 VINEYARD.

Rev. JAMES CARTER, 1894, 1897.

1. Thrice the mas-ter hast-ened To the mark-et-place; Thrice found wait-ing workmen With ex-pect-ant face. "Where-fore stand ye i-dle?" Did he chid-ing say, "Go in-to the vine-yard; Fill the wan-ing day."

Refrain.
Why stand ye all the day i-dle! Work in a-bund-ance a-waits. Gath-er the clus-ters of har-vest, Bear them in joy thro' the gates.

Words and Music Copyright, 1894, 1899, by Rev. James Carter.

2 Go into the vineyard,
  Ye who dwell at ease;
 E'en the Lord Christ sought not
  His own Self to please.
 Trod the lowly Master
  Ways defiled and dim,
 Shall His ransomed servant
  Fail to follow Him?

3 Swift the sands are flowing;
  Life is flying fast;
 Soon the day of working
  Will be wholly past.
 Where are all the trophies
  You once thought to bring
 As you planned and pondered
  In life's dreamy spring?

Rev. James Carter, 1894.

THE BANNER OF HIS LOVE

194 LABARUM. S. M. With Refrain. Rev. JAMES CARTER, 1895.

2 There are lights that falsely shine,
　There are shades where tempters hide ;
　But above us gleams the holy sign
　　Of our Saviour crucified.

3 With a purpose firm and high,
　With endeavor brave and strong ;
　If we simply trust and truly try,
　　We shall triumph o'er the wrong.

4 By our Captain's great command,
　By the word we must obey,
　Let us each outreach a helping hand
　　To the lost along the way.

5 Brothers, let us bravely fight ;
　Brothers, let us gladly sing ;
　Till we catch the light and climb the hight
　　To the city of our King.

Emma Smuller Carter, 1895.

ONWARD IN HIS NAME.

195 PROCLAMATION. 6.5. 12 1. Rev. JAMES CARTER. 1-95.

1. For-ward, Host of Heav-en, Harnessed for the fight; Je-sus' cross, your ban-ner; Je-sus' word, your light. On through mist and shad-ow, On through storm and heat, Till you lay your tro-phies At your Captain's feet. Ar-my of En-deav-or, One in hope and aim, On the world to res-cue, On-ward in His Name.

Words and Music Copyright, 1899, by Rev. James Carter.

2 Purer yet and truer,
  Battling for the right,
Mount, O Host of Jesus,
  Up the steeps of light.
Smite the tents of evil;
  Flare your torches wide,
Till the hosts of Satan
  Know not where to hide.

3 Onward, ever onward,
  March, O Host of light,
On to free the nations
  Shadowed still in night.
Break the chains of darkness,
  Set the captives free;
Teach the slaves of Satan
  Christ's glad liberty.

Rev. James Carter, 1895.

SHINING AS LIGHTS.

196 SUNSHINE.

Rev. JAMES CARTER, 1895.

1. Let the light that is in you be shining, The faith that upholds you be known, With the love of the Saviour combining To prove He has made you His own.

Refrain.
Shining, shining, Shine forth the light of the gospel of Jesus Over the darkness of sin...... Let the light that is in you be shining Lost souls unto Jesus to win.

2 Let the truth that you cherish be glowing
　In courage and energy bright;
With the face of an angel be showing
　We herald a gospel of light.

3 Let the joy that Christ gives you forever
　His praise 'mid earth's dissonance sing;
Let each evening record an endeavor
　Some soul to His kingdom to bring.

4 With the message of gladness enlighten,
　A joy and a comforter be,
Till eternity's morning shall brighten
　And sorrow and sighing shall flee.

Rev. James Carter, 1895.

GO YE INTO ALL THE WORLD.

2 Go for cleansing, go for healing,
  Go to him whose need is sore;
  Go, the risen Lord revealing,
  Living, loving evermore.

3 Tell the slaves of sin, how Jesus
  Bids our sinful bondage cease;
  How He loves us, how He frees us,
  Gives us pardon, power, and peace.

4 Go among the high and lowly,
  To the sinful and the sad;
  Tell them Christ can make them holy;
  Tell them Christ will make them glad.

Emma Smuller Carter, 1895.

198 ANGELUS. L. M.
GEORG JOSEPHI, 1655.

1. Lord, speak to me, that I may speak
In living echoes of Thy tone;
As Thou hast sought, so let me seek
Thy erring children lost and lone.

2 Oh, lead me, Lord, that I may lead
  The wandering and the wavering feet;
Oh, feed me, Lord, that I may feed
  Thy hungering ones with manna sweet.

3 Oh, strengthen me, that while I stand
  Firm on the Rock, and strong in Thee,
I may stretch out a loving hand
  To wrestlers with the troubled sea.

4 Oh, teach me, Lord, that I may teach
  The precious things Thou dost impart;
And wing my words, that they may reach
  The hidden depths of many a heart.

5 Oh, give Thine own sweet rest to me,
  That I may speak with soothing power
A word in season, as from Thee,
  To weary ones in needful hour.

6 Oh, use me, Lord, use even me,
  Just as Thou wilt, and when, and where;
Until Thy blessèd face I see,
  Thy rest, Thy joy, Thy glory share.
      Frances Ridley Havergal, 1872.

199 QUEBEC. L. M.
Rev. Sir HENRY WILLIAMS BAKER, 1866.

1. Go, labor on, while it is day,
The world's dark night is hast'ning on;
Speed, speed thy work, cast sloth away;
It is not thus that souls are won.

2 Men die in darkness at your side,
  Without a hope to cheer the tomb;
Take up the torch and wave it wide,
  The torch that lights time's thickest gloom.

3 Toil on, faint not, keep watch and pray;
  Be wise the erring soul to win;
Go forth into the world's highway,
  Compel the wanderer to come in.

4 Go, labor on; your hands are weak,
  Your knees are faint, your soul cast down,
Yet falter not; the prize you seek
  Is near,—a kingdom and a crown!
      Rev. Horatius Bonar, 1843.

CONQUERING AND TO CONQUER.

200 CONFLICT. 8. 8. 8. 7. D.

GIOACHINO ANTONIO ROSSINI, 1815.
Arr. by C. ARTHUR JACQUES, 1894.

1. Thro' the conflict of the ages, Where the host of Satan rages, Christ with all His saints engages In the tumult of the war.

Refrain.
Forward, Christian, forward ever; Christ forsakes His faithful never, But His host of high endeavor Leads to triumph evermore.

2 Called to serve from every nation,
Called to holy consecration,
Ours the lofty imitation
Of the Lord whom we adore.

3 Trusted with the great commission,
Let it be our high ambition
To proclaim His free remission
To the Christless at our door.

4 Till the roar of battle endeth,
And the Lord in clouds descendeth,
Till His host triumphant blendeth
With the great host gone before.

Rev. James Carter, 1894.

---

201 (QUEBEC). L. M.

1 Go, labor on; spend and be spent,—
  Thy joy to do the Father's will;
  It is the way the Master went,
  Should not the servant tread it still?

2 Go, labor on; 'tis not for naught;
  Thine earthly loss is heavenly gain;
  Men heed thee, love thee, praise thee not;
  The Master praises,—what are men?

3 Go, labor on; enough, while here,
  If He shall praise thee, if He deign
  Thy willing heart to mark and cheer;
  No toil for Him shall be in vain.

4 Toil on, and in thy toil rejoice;
  For toil comes rest, for exile home;
  Soon shalt thou hear the Bridegroom's voice,
  The midnight peal, "Behold, I come!"

Rev. Horatius Bonar, 1843.

SOWING IN TEARS.

202 STOCKWELL. 8. 7.
Rev. DARIUS ELIOT JONES, 1848.

1. He that go-eth forth with weep-ing, Bear-ing pre-cious seed in love,
Nev-er tir-ing, nev-er sleep-ing, Find-eth mer-cy from a-bove.

2 Soft descend the dews of Heaven,
Bright the rays celestial shine;
Precious fruits will thus be given,
Through an influence all divine.

3 Sow thy seed, be never weary,
Let no fears thy soul annoy;
Be the prospect ne'er so dreary,
Thou shalt reap the fruits of joy.
Thomas Hastings, 1836.

203 DUKE STREET. L. M.
JOHN HATTON, c. 1790.

1. Take up thy cross, the Sav-iour said, If thou wouldst My dis-ci-ple be;
De-ny thy-self, the world for-sake, And humbly fol-low aft-er Me.

2 Take up thy cross; let not its weight
Fill thy weak spirit with alarm;
His strength shall bear thy spirit up,
And brace thy heart, and nerve thine arm.

3 Take up thy cross, nor heed the shame,
Nor let thy foolish pride rebel:
Thy Lord for thee the cross endured,
To save thy soul from death and hell.

4 Take up thy cross, and follow Christ,
Nor think till death to lay it down;
For only he who bears the cross,
May hope to wear the starry crown.
Rev. Charles William Everest, 1833. Ab. and alt.

204

1 So let our lips and lives express
The holy gospel, we profess;
So let our works and virtues shine,
To prove the doctrine all divine.

2 Thus shall we best proclaim abroad
The honors of our Saviour God;
When His salvation reigns within,
And grace subdues the power of sin.

3 Religion bears our spirits up,
While we expect that blessed hope,—
The bright appearance of the Lord:
And faith stands leaning on His word.
Rev. Isaac Watts, 1709. Ab.

TO THE WORK.

205 ST. AGNES. C. M. Rev. JOHN BACCHUS DYKES, 1852.

1. Scorn not the slight-est word or deed, Nor deem it void of pow'r;
There's fruit in each wind-waft-ed seed, That waits its na-tal hour.

2 A whispered word may touch the heart,
And call it back to life;
A look of love bid sin depart,
And still unholy strife.

3 No act falls fruitless; none can tell
How vast its power may be,
Nor what results infolded dwell
Within it silently.

4 Work on, despair not, bring thy mite,
Nor care how small it be;
God is with all that serve the right,
The holy, true, and free.

English Author, 1845.

206 WIMBORNE. 9. 8. JOHN WHITAKER, 1849.

Words Copyright, 1894, by Rev. James Carter.

1. See yonder stands the wheat un-bro-ken, Ripe for the reap-er waves the grain;
Heed the command the Lord hath spo-ken: Go, reap;—no toil for Him is vain.

2 Many the tracts in God's broad acres
Where ripened grain falls to decay;
Sad as a ship 'mid angry breakers,
Drifting to wreck in open day.

3 O child of God, the souls that perish
Are sometimes not beyond the sea!
Christ calls thee His lost sheep to cherish
Whose lives unsaved are nearest thee.

4 Oh! may this thought thy heart embolden,
Stirring thy soul from sinful ease,
Thy Saviour's word: "From Me withholden,
Was whatsoe'er ye held from these."

5 Go forth, O coward soul, to gather
What sheaves await thy sickle's swing;
There meet with dreaded failure rather
Than fail to serve the Saviour King.

6 Go, lay thy life upon the altar;
God will accept the sacrifice;
Forth to the work, and never falter;
Tarries for thee the heavenly prize.

Rev. James Carter, 1894.

CHRISTIAN ACTIVITY.

207 ENSIGN. L. M.   JOHN BAPTISTE CALKIN, 1872.

1. Fling out the banner: let it float Skyward and seaward, high and wide; The sun that lights its shining folds, The cross, on which the Saviour died.

2 Fling out the banner: angels bend
    In anxious silence o'er the sign,
  And vainly seek to comprehend
    The wonder of the Love divine.

3 Fling out the banner: heathen lands
    Shall see from far the glorious sight;
  And nations, crowding to be born,
    Baptize their spirits in its light.

4 Fling out the banner: let it float
    Skyward and seaward, high and wide:
  Our glory only in the cross,
    Our only hope, the Crucified.

5 Fling out the banner: wide and high,
    Skyward and seaward let it shine;
  Nor skill, nor might, nor merit ours;
    We conquer only in that sign.

                          Bp. George Washington Doane, 1848.

208 RENOVATION. S. M.   JOHANN NEPOMUK HUMMEL, 1832.

1. We give Thee but Thine own, What-e'er the gift may be: All that we have is Thine alone, A trust, O Lord, from Thee.

2 May we Thy bounties thus
    As stewards true receive;
  And gladly, as Thou blessest us,
    To Thee our first-fruits give.

3 And we believe Thy word,
    Though dim our faith may be;
  Whate'er for Thine we do, O Lord,
    We do it unto Thee.

          Bp. William Walsham How, 1858. Ab.

209

1 The harvest dawn is near,
    The year delays not long;
  And he who sows with many a tear,
    Shall reap with many a song.

2 Sad to his toil he goes,
    His seed with weeping leaves;
  But he shall come, at twilight's close,
    And bring his golden sheaves.

          Bp. George Burgess, 1839. Ab.

2 Show us where we have omitted
   To fulfill the moment's duty;
   Fill us with Thy heavenly beauty;
   Make us temples worthy Thee.
 May our waiting hearts be fitted
   For the conflict close before us;
   May Thy banner floating o'er us
   Guidon and protection be.

3 Lord accept our consecration;
   May Thy love possess us wholly;
   Make us earnest, make us lowly;
   May Thy Spirit rule alone.
 Fill with higher aspiration;
   Win through us the sheep that wander;
   Use us as Thou wilt, till yonder
   We rejoice before Thy throne.

Rev. James Carter, 1894.

FAREWELL AND RECEPTION.

212 ENDEAVOR. 8. 7. D. Rev. JAMES CARTER, 1891.

1. May the God of peace watch o'er you,
   Fellow soldier in the fight,
   May His angel go before you,
   Guide you in the path of light.

   Refrain.
   Meet we here, or meet we never
   Till the day that shines forever,
   May God bless your faith's endeavor,
   Give you vict'ry evermore.

Words and Music Copyright, 1894, by Rev. James Carter.

Benediction Hymn.

2 May the God of battles send you
  Succor swift in danger's hour;
  May His arm of might defend you
  From the tempter's fatal power.

3 May the love of Christ constrain you
  Still to live for Him who died;
  May the might of faith maintain you
  Spotless in the Crucified.

4 So at last, the conflict ended,
  And the battered shield laid down,
  To the City Gates ascended,
  May you wear the victor's crown.

Rev. James Carter, 1891.

---

213 (ST. ALPHEGE). 7. 6.

Reception of Members.

1 We stand to bid you welcome
  As fellow-workers true;
  We hope to help you onward,
  We look for help from you.

2 Hold fast your heavenly treasure;
  Stand fast in Christ, the Lord,
  Supported by His presence,
  Enlightened by His word.

3 Lord Jesus, keep Thy soldiers,
  Through all the holy war;
  And lead them on triumphant
  To rest for evermore.

Rev. James Carter, 1894.

LOVE FOR THE CHURCH.

214 STATE STREET. S. M.
JONATHAN CALL WOODMAN, 1844.

1. I love Thy kingdom, Lord,— The house of Thine abode, The Church our blest Redeemer saved With His own precious blood.

2 I love Thy Church, O God!
  Her walls before Thee stand,
Dear as the apple of Thine eye,
  And graven on Thy hand.

3 For her my tears shall fall,
  For her my prayers ascend;
To her my cares and toils be given,
  Till toils and cares shall end.

4 Beyond my highest joy
  I prize her heavenly ways,
Her sweet communion, solemn vows,
  Her hymns of love and praise.

5 Sure as Thy truth shall last,
  To Zion shall be given
The brightest glories earth can yield,
  And brighter bliss of Heaven.

Rev. Timothy Dwight, 1800. Ab.

215 DENNIS. S. M.
JOHANN GEORG NÄGELI, 1832.
Arr. by LOWELL MASON, 1845.

1. Blest be the tie that binds Our hearts in Christian love: The fellowship of kindred minds Is like to that above.

2 Before our Father's throne
  We pour our ardent prayers;
Our fears, our hopes, our aims are one,
  Our comforts and our cares.

3 We share our mutual woes,
  Our mutual burdens bear;
And often for each other flows
  The sympathizing tear.

4 When we asunder part,
  It gives us inward pain;
But we shall still be joined in heart,
  And hope to meet again.

5 From sorrow, toil, and pain,
  And sin, we shall be free,
And perfect love and friendship reign
  Through all eternity.

Rev. John Fawcett, 1772. Ab.

A GLORIOUS CHURCH.

216 FALFIELD. 8.7. D.   Sir. ARTHUR SEYMOUR SULLIVAN, 1867.

1. Glorious things of thee are spoken, Zion, city of our God! He whose word cannot be broken, Formed thee for His own abode: On the Rock of Ages founded—What can shake thy sure repose? With salvation's walls surrounded, Thou may'st smile at all thy foes.

2 See, the streams of living waters,
  Springing from eternal love,
Well supply thy sons and daughters,
  And all fear of want remove:
Who can faint, while such a river
  Ever flows their thirst t' assuage?
Grace, which, like the Lord, the giver,
  Never fails from age to age.

3 Round each habitation hovering,
  See the cloud and fire appear!
For a glory and a covering,
  Showing that the Lord is near:
Thus deriving from their banner
  Light by night and shade by day,
Safe they feed upon the manna,
  Which He gives them when they pray.
          Rev. John Newton, 1779. Ab.

217

1 Through the night of doubt and sorrow
  Onward goes the pilgrim band,
Singing songs of expectation,
  Marching to the promised land.
Clear before us, through the darkness
  Gleams and burns the guiding light:
Brother clasps the hand of brother,
  Stepping fearless through the night.

2 One the strain the lips of thousands
  Lift as from the heart of one;
One the conflict, one the peril,
  One the march in God begun:
One the gladness of rejoicing
  On the far eternal shore,
Where the one almighty Father,
  Reigns in love for evermore.
        Bernhardt Severin Ingemann, 1825.
  Tr. by Rev. Sabine Baring-Gould, 1867, 1875. Ab.

THE CHURCH OF CHRIST.

218 ST. ANN'S. C. M. WILLIAM CROFT, 1708.

1. Oh, where are kings and empires now, Of old that went and came? But, Lord, Thy Church is praying yet, A thousand years the same.

2 We mark her goodly battlements,
   And her foundations strong;
  We hear within the solemn voice
   Of her unending song.
3 For not like kingdoms of the world
   Thy holy Church, O God!
  Though earthquake shocks are threatening
   And tempests are abroad;— [her,
4 Unshaken as eternal hills,
   Immovable she stands,
  A mountain that shall fill the earth,
   A house not made by hands.
                    Bp. Arthur Cleveland Coxe, 1839. Alt.

219 DEDHAM. C. M. WILLIAM GARDINER, c. 1820.

1. Let saints below in concert sing With those to glory gone; For all the servants of our King In earth and Heav'n are one.

2 One family, we dwell in Him,
   One Church above, beneath,
  Though now divided by the stream,
   The narrow stream of death;—
3 One army of the living God,
   To His command we bow;
  Part of the host have crossed the flood,
   And part are crossing now.
4 Ev'n now to their eternal home
   Some happy spirits fly;
  And we are to the margin come,
   And soon expect to die.
5 Ev'n now, by faith, we join our hands
   With those that went before,
  And greet the ransomed blessèd bands
   Upon th' eternal shore.
6 Lord Jesus! be our constant guide:
   And, when the word is given,
  Bid death's cold flood its waves divide,
   And land us safe in Heaven.
                    Rev. Charles Wesley, 1759. Ab. and alt.

THE CHILDREN OF THE COVENANT.

220 AZMON. C. M. CARL GOTTHELF GLÄSER, 1828.
Arr. by LOWELL MASON, 1839.

1. O God of Beth-el, by whose hand Thy people still are fed;
Who thro' this weary pilgrimage Hast all our fathers led!

2 Our vows, our prayers, we now present
  Before Thy throne of grace;
  God of our fathers! be the God
  Of their succeeding race.

3 Through each perplexing path of life
  Our wandering footsteps guide;
  Give us, each day, our daily bread,
  And raiment fit provide.

4 Oh, spread Thy covering wings around,
  Till all our wanderings cease,
  And at our Father's loved abode,
  Our souls arrive in peace.

  Rev. Philip Doddridge, 1737.
  Rev. John Logan, 1781. Alt. and ab.

221 SILOAM. C. M. ISAAC BAKER WOODBURY, 1842.

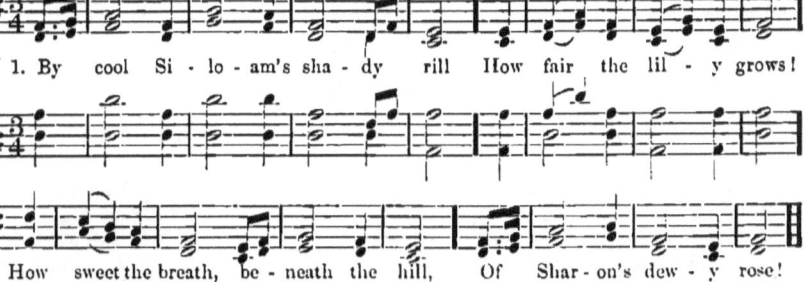

1. By cool Siloam's shady rill How fair the lily grows!
How sweet the breath, beneath the hill, Of Sharon's dewy rose!

2 Lo! such the child whose early feet
  The paths of peace have trod;
  Whose secret heart, with influence sweet,
  Is upward drawn to God.

3 By cool Siloam's shady rill
  The lily must decay;
  The rose that blooms beneath the hill
  Must shortly fade away.

4 And soon, too soon, the wintry hour
  Of man's maturer age
  May shake the soul with sorrow's power
  And stormy passion's rage.

5 O Thou, whose infant feet were found
  Within Thy Father's shrine, [crowned,
  Whose years, with changeless virtue
  Were all alike divine!

6 Dependent on Thy bounteous breath,
  We seek Thy grace alone
  In childhood, manhood, age and death,
  To keep us still Thine own.

  Bp. Reginald Heber, 1812, 1827.

AT THE CROSS.

222 BASEL. Rev. James Carter, 1895.

1. Once more the feast of love is spread,
Once more the guests are bidden;
O Lord, who art the broken Bread,
The heav'nly Manna hidden,
Reveal to us the mystery,
Thine inward vision giving,
That through the symbol we may see
The Saviour, dying, living.

2 O Lamb of God, Thy blood apply,
Prepare each waiting spirit;
Oh, pardon Thou, and purify,
And cover with Thy merit.
No safeguard have we but the sign
Thy sacrifice revealing;
No life but through Thy death divine,
No health but through Thy healing.

3 Set free our souls from bonds of sin,
That all too long have bound us,
Let each anew the race begin,
Thine arm of strength around us.
May we with searching glance this day
Cast out all sinful leaven;
And gird us for the onward way
Fed by the Bread of Heaven.

Emma Smuller Carter, 1895.

---

223 (BEATITUDE). C. M.

1 According to Thy gracious word,
In meek humility,
This will I do, my dying Lord,
I will remember Thee.

2 When to the cross I turn mine eyes,
And rest on Calvary,
O Lamb of God, my Sacrifice!
I must remember Thee:—

3 Remember Thee, and all Thy pains
And all Thy love to me;
Yea, while a breath, a pulse remains,
Will I remember Thee.

4 And when these failing lips grow dumb,
And mind and memory flee,
When Thou shalt in Thy kingdom come,
Then, Lord, remember me!

James Montgomery, 1825. Ab.

BEFORE THE CROSS.

224 WHITAKER. 8. 7. D. FRIEDRICH FREIHERR VON FLOTOW, 1847. Arr. by C. ARTHUR JACQUES, 1898.

1. Sweet the mo-ments, rich in bless-ing, Which be-fore the cross I spend;
Life, and health, and peace pos-sess-ing, From the sin-ner's dy-ing Friend.
D. S.—drops, my soul be-dew-ing, Plead and claim my peace with God.
Here I'll sit, for ev-er view-ing Mer-cy's streams in streams of blood; Pre-cious

2 Truly blessèd is this station,
  Low before His cross to lie,
While I see divine compassion,
  Floating in His languid eye.
Love and grief my heart dividing,
  With my tears His feet I bathe;
Constant still, in faith abiding,
  Life deriving from His death.

3 Here I feel my sins forgiven,
  While upon the Lamb I gaze,
And my thoughts are all of Heaven,
  And my lips o'erflow with praise.
Still in ceaseless contemplation,
  Fix my heart and eyes on Thee,
Till I taste Thy full salvation,
  And, unvailed, Thy glories see.
      Rev. James Allen, 1757.
      Rev. Walter Shirley, 1770. Alt.

BEATITUDE. C. M. Rev. JOHN BACCHUS DYKES, 1875.

1. Ac-cord-ing to Thy gra-cious word, In meek hu-mil-i-ty,
This will I do, my dy-ing Lord, I will re-mem-ber Thee.

BENEATH HIS SHADOW.

225 AURELIA. 7. 6. D. SAMUEL SEBASTIAN WESLEY, c. 1865.

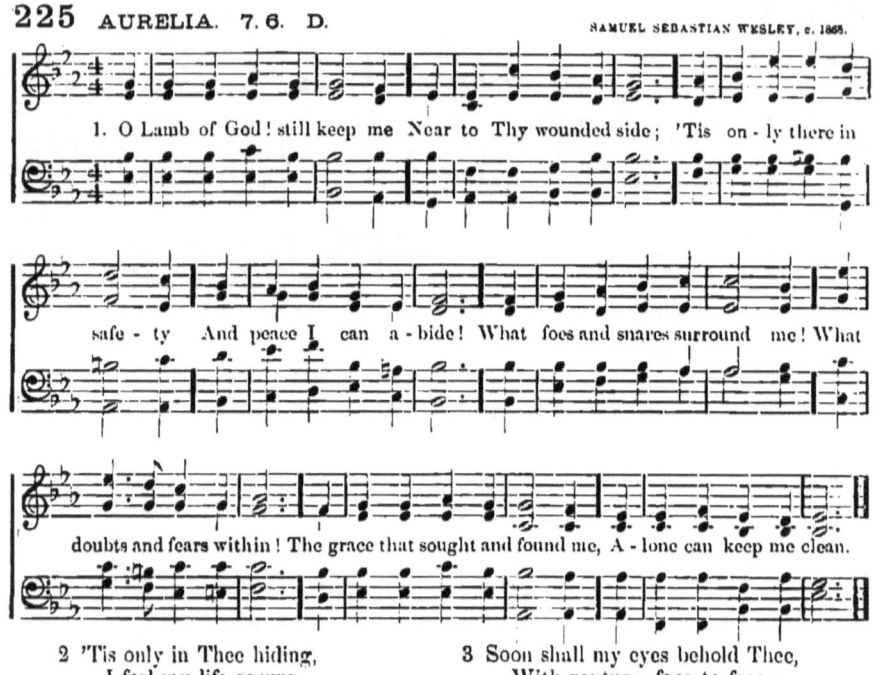

1. O Lamb of God! still keep me Near to Thy wounded side; 'Tis on-ly there in safe-ty And peace I can a-bide! What foes and snares surround me! What doubts and fears within! The grace that sought and found me, A-lone can keep me clean.

2 'Tis only in Thee hiding,
   I feel my life secure—
Only in Thee abiding,
   The conflict can endure:
Thine arm the victory gaineth
   O'er every hateful foe;
Thy love my heart sustaineth
   In all its care and woe.

3 Soon shall my eyes behold Thee,
   With rapture, face to face;
One half hath not been told me
   Of all Thy power and grace:
Thy beauty, Lord, and glory,
   The wonders of Thy love,
Shall be the endless story
   Of all Thy saints above.

James George Deck, 1842.

ST. ALPHEGE. 7. 6. HENRY JOHN GAUNTLETT, 1852.

1. Sit down be-neath His shad-ow, And rest with great de-light; The faith that now be-holds Him Is pledge of fu-ture sight.

CONTEMPLATION OF CHRIST.

226 PASSION CHORALE. 7. 6. D.
HANS LEO HASSLER, 1601.
Harmonized by JOHANN SEBASTIAN BACH, 1729.

1. O sacred Head, now wounded, With grief and shame weighed down,
Now scornfully surrounded, With thorns Thine only crown;
O sacred Head, what glory, What bliss, till now was Thine!
Yet, though despised and gory, I joy to call Thee mine.

2 What Thou, my Lord, hast suffered
  Was all for sinners' gain:
Mine, mine was the transgression,
  But Thine the deadly pain:
Lo, here I fall, my Saviour!
  'Tis I deserve Thy place;
Look on me with Thy favor,
  Vouchsafe to me Thy grace.

3 What language shall I borrow,
  To thank Thee, dearest Friend:
For this, Thy dying sorrow,
  Thy pity without end?

Lord, make me Thine forever,
  Nor let me faithless prove:
Oh! let me never, never,
  Abuse such dying love.

4 Be near me when I'm dying,
  Oh! show Thy cross to me!
And for my succor flying,
  Come, Lord, and set me free!
These eyes, new faith receiving,
  From Jesus shall not move;
For he who dies believing,
  Dies safely—through Thy love.

Bernard of Clairvaux.
Rev. Paul Gerhardt, 1659.
Rev. James Waddell Alexander, 1820. Ab.

---

227 (ST. ALPHEGE). 7. 6.

1 Sit down beneath His shadow,
  And rest with great delight;
The faith that now beholds Him
  Is pledge of future sight.

2 Our Master's love remember,
  Exceeding great and free;
Lift up thy heart in gladness,
  For He remembers thee.

3 Bring every weary burden,
  Thy sin, thy fear, thy grief;
He calls the heavy laden
  And gives them kind relief.

4 His righteousness "all glorious"
  Thy festal robe shall be;
And love that passeth knowledge
  His banner over thee.

5 A little while, though parted,
  Remember, wait, and love,
Until He comes in glory,
  Until we meet above.

6 Till in the Father's kingdom
  The heavenly feast is spread,
And we behold His beauty,
  Whose blood for us was shed!

Miss Frances Ridley Havergal, 1870.

BEFORE THE CROSS.

228 EUCHARIST. 11.10.
Rev. JAMES CARTER, 1892.

1. Come ye yourselves apart in desert places, Where, toil-worn, burdened, or by care oppressed, Ye may find respite from earth's thronging faces; Your Master bids you, Come apart and rest.

2 Come ye, and view the mystery unfolden:
That thorn-crowned Head for your transgression torn,
That Body bruised, upon the cross upholden,
That Holy One who all your stripes hath borne.

3 Come ye yourselves apart; the holy vision
Constrain each soul to live for Him who died,
Strengthen to front temptation and derision,
Spotless and blameless thro' the Crucified.

4 Where seraphs vail with wings of flame their faces,—
Holy the Presence; naught can there defile,—
Come ye, and sit with Christ in heavenly places;
Come ye yourselves apart and rest awhile.

Rev. James Carter, 1889.

ESHTEMOA. 7.
TIMOTHY BATTLE MASON, 1852.

1. Thine for-ev-er! God of love, Hear us from Thy throne above! Thine for-ev-er may we be, Here, and in e-ter-ni-ty!

THE LORD'S SUPPER.

229 ZEPHYR. L. M.
WILLIAM BATCHELDER BRADBURY, 1844.

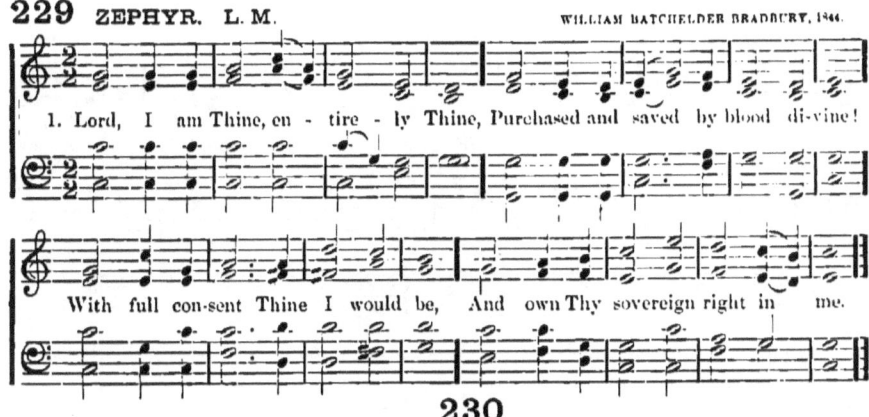

1. Lord, I am Thine, en-tire-ly Thine, Purchased and saved by blood di-vine!
With full con-sent Thine I would be, And own Thy sovereign right in me.

2 Grant one poor sinner more a place,
Among the children of Thy grace;
A wretched sinner, lost to God,
But ransomed by Immanuel's blood.

3 Thine would I live, Thine would I die,
Be Thine through all eternity;
The vow is passed beyond repeal;
Now will I set the solemn seal.

4 Here at that cross where flows the blood
That bought my guilty soul for God;
Thee, my new Master, now I call,
And consecrate to Thee my all.

5 Do Thou assist a feeble worm,
The great engagement to perform;
Thy grace can full assistance lend,
And on that grace I dare depend.
Rev. Samuel Davies, 1769. Ab.

230
1 Draw near, O Holy Dove, draw near,
With peace and gladness on Thy wing;
Reveal the Saviour's presence here,
And light, and life, and comfort bring.

2 "Eat, O my friends—drink, O beloved!"
We hear the Master's voice exclaim:
Our hearts with new desire are moved,
And kindled with a heavenly flame.

3 No room for doubt, no room for dread,
Nor tears, nor groans, nor anxious sighs;
We do not mourn a Saviour dead,
But hail Him living in the skies.

4 While this we do, remembering Thee,
Dear Saviour, let our graces prove
We have Thy blessed company,
Thy banner over us is love.
Rev. Aaron Robarts Wolfe, 1858.

231 (ESHTEMOA). 7.
1 Thine for ever! God of love,
Hear us from Thy throne above!
Thine for ever may we be,
Here and in eternity!

2 Thine forever! Lord of Life,
Shield us through our earthly strife;
Thou, the Life, the Truth, the Way,
Guide us to the realms of day.

3 Thine forever! oh, how blest
They who find in Thee their rest!
Saviour, Guardian, heavenly Friend,
Oh, defend us to the end!

4 Thine forever! Thou our Guide,—
All our wants by Thee supplied,
All our sins by Thee forgiven,
Lead us, Lord, from earth to Heaven!
Mary Fawler Maude, 1847. Ab.

232 7.
1 When on Sinai's top I see
God descend, in majesty,
To proclaim His holy law,
All my spirit sinks with awe.

2 When in ecstacy sublime,
Hermon's glorious steep I climb,
At the too transporting light,
Darkness rushes o'er my sight.

3 When on Calvary I rest,
God, in flesh made manifest,
Shines in my Redeemer's face,
Full of beauty, truth, and grace.

4 Here I would forever stay,
Weep and gaze my soul away;
Thou art Heaven on earth to me,
Lovely, mournful Calvary!
Rev. James Montgomery, 1812.

THE UNIVERSAL PROCLAMATION.

233 MISSIONARY HYMN. 7. 6. D. LOWELL MASON, 1823.

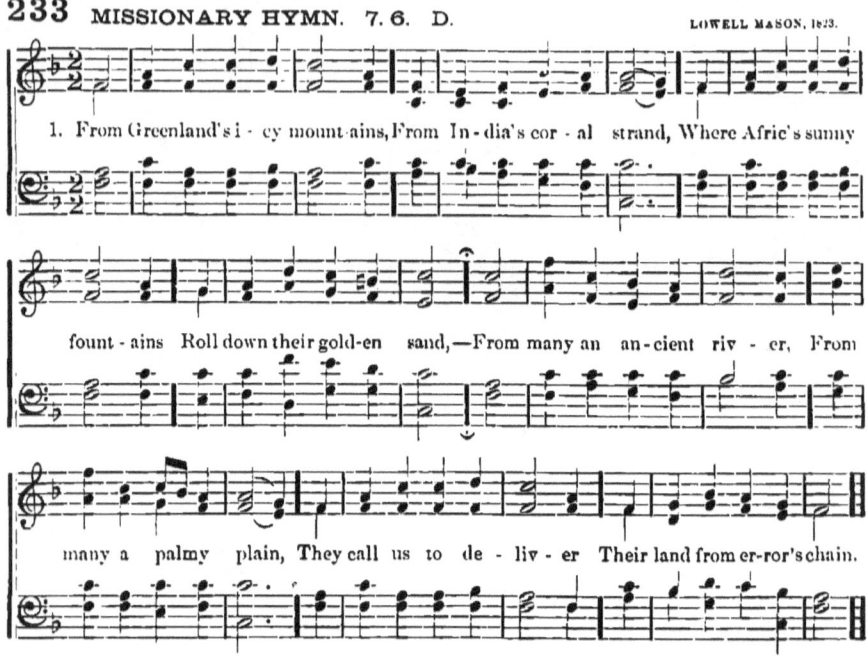

1. From Greenland's i-cy mountains, From In-dia's cor-al strand, Where Afric's sunny fount-ains Roll down their gold-en sand,—From many an an-cient riv-er, From many a palmy plain, They call us to de-liv-er Their land from er-ror's chain.

2 What though the spicy breezes
  Blow soft o'er Ceylon's isle;
 Though every prospect pleases,
  And only man is vile;
 In vain with lavish kindness
  The gifts of God are strown;
 The heathen, in his blindness,
  Bows down to wood and stone!

3 Shall we, whose souls are lighted
  With wisdom from on high,—
 Shall we, to men benighted,
  The lamp of life deny?
 Salvation, oh, salvation!
  The joyful sound proclaim,
 Till earth's remotest nation
  Has learned Messiah's Name.

4 Waft, waft, ye winds, His story,
  And you, ye waters, roll,
 Till, like a sea of glory,
  It spreads from pole to pole;
 Till o'er our ransomed nature
  The Lamb for sinners slain,
 Redeemer, King, Creator,
  In bliss returns to reign!
  Bp. Reginald Heber, 1819.

234

1 Hail to the Lord's Anointed,
  Great David's greater Son!
 Hail, in the time appointed,
  His reign on earth begun!
 He comes to break oppression,
  To set the captive free,
 To take away transgression,
  And rule in equity.

2 He comes, with succor speedy,
  To those who suffer wrong;
 To help the poor and needy,
  And bid the weak be strong;
 To give them songs for sighing,
  Their darkness turn to light,
 Whose souls, condemned and dying,
  Were precious in His sight.

3 For Him shall prayer unceasing
  And daily vows ascend;
 His kingdom still increasing,
  A kingdom without end.
 The tide of time shall never
  His covenant remove;
 His Name shall stand for ever;
  His great, best Name of Love!
  James Montgomery, 1821. Al.

MESSIAH'S CONQUEST.

235 GLADNESS. 7.6. D.   JOSEPH BARNBY, 1868.

1. O Love Divine, who seek-est The sheep that wander far, The wil-ful-est and weak-est, Though marked by many a scar, And, where-so-e'er they wan-der On mountains drear and cold, In love, than all loves fon-der, Dost bring them to the fold,—

2 Thy people's supplication
  In favor Thou hast heard,
And Thou hast wrought salvation,
  And magnified Thy word.
Thy joyful people bless Thee;
  Thy faithfulness they sing
For those who now confess Thee,
  Their gracious Lord and King.

3 To Thee whose throne of splendor
  The angel myriads throng,
Thy battling legions render
  The homage of their song,
And round Thy cross assemble
  To praise Thy triumphs bright,—
The Law which made them tremble,
  Transformed to love and light.

4 O Lord of life, victorious
  Upon Thy Father's throne,
Thy triumph shall be glorious,
  The universe Thine own.
Thy saints shall tell the story
  On the eternal shore,
And Thy domain of glory
  Increase forevermore.
        Rev. James Carter, 1896.

236

1 The morning light is breaking;
  The darkness disappears!
The sons of earth are waking
  To penitential tears;
Each breeze that sweeps the ocean
  Brings tidings from afar,
Of nations in commotion,
  Prepared for Zion's war.

2 See heathen nations bending
  Before the God we love,
And thousand hearts ascending
  In gratitude above;
While sinners, now confessing,
  The gospel call obey,
And seek the Saviour's blessing—
  A nation in a day.

3 Blest river of salvation!
  Pursue thine onward way;
Flow thou to every nation,
  Nor in thy richness stay:
Stay not till all the lowly
  Triumphant reach their home:
Stay not till all the holy
  Proclaim—"The Lord is come!"
      Rev. Samuel Francis Smith, 1832. Ab.

THE UNIVERSAL CONQUEST.

237 MISSIONARY CHANT. L. M.
HEINRICH CHRISTOPHER ZEUNER, 1832.

1. Jesus shall reign where'er the sun
Does His successive journeys run;
His kingdom stretch from shore to shore,
Till moons shall wax and wane no more.

2 For Him shall endless prayer be made,
And praises throng to crown His head;
His Name, like sweet perfume, shall rise
With every morning sacrifice.

3 People and realms of every tongue
Dwell on His love with sweetest song;
And infant voices shall proclaim
Their early blessings on His Name.

4 Blessings abound where'er He reigns,
The prisoner leaps to lose his chains;
The weary find eternal rest,
And all the sons of want are blest.

5 Let every creature rise, and bring
Peculiar honors to our King:
Angels descend with songs again,
And earth repeat the long amen.
Rev. Isaac Watts, 1719. Ab.

238

1 O Spirit of the living God,
In all Thy plenitude of grace,
Where'er the foot of man hath trod,
Descend on our apostate race.

2 Give tongues of fire, and hearts of love,
To preach the reconciling word;
Give power and unction from above,
Where'er the joyful sound is heard.

3 Be darkness, at Thy coming, light:
Confusion—order, in Thy path;
Souls without strength, inspire with might;
Bid mercy triumph over wrath.

4 Baptize the nations, far and nigh;
The triumphs of the cross record;
The name of Jesus glorify,
Till every kindred call Him Lord.
James Montgomery, 1823. Ab.

HOLY CROSS. C. M.
JOHANN C. W. A. MOZART. [?]
Arr. by JAMES CLIFFT WADE, 1870.

1. My feet are weary with the march Over the steep hill-side;
City of God! I fain would see Thy peaceful waters glide!

NEARER HOME.

239 LEOMINSTER. S. M. D.
GEORGE WILLIAM MARTIN, 1862.
Har. by Sir ARTHUR SEYMOUR SULLIVAN, 1874.
Slowly.

1. One sweetly solemn thought Comes to me o'er and o'er,
That I am nearer home today Than e'er I've been before;
Nearer my Father's house, Where many mansions be;
Nearer today the great white throne, Nearer the crystal sea;—

2 Nearer the bound of life,
　Where burdens are laid down;
Nearer to leave the painful cross;
　Nearer to gain the crown.
But, lying dark between,
　Winding down through the night,
There rolls the silent, unknown stream
　That leads at last to light.

3 It may be that my feet
　Are slipping o'er the brink,
It may be I am nearer home,—
　Nearer than now I think.
Father, perfect my trust!
　Strengthen the might of faith!
Nor let me stand, at last, alone
　Upon the shore of death.
　　　　　Miss Phœbe Cary, 1852. Ab.

---

240 (HOLY CROSS). C. M.

1 My feet are weary with the march
　Over the steep hill-side;
City of God! I fain would see
　Thy peaceful waters glide!

2 My hands are weary, toiling on
　For perishable meat;
City of God! I fain would reach
　Thy glorious mercy-seat!

3 Patience, poor heart! His feet were worn,
　His hands were weary too;
His garments stained, and travel-torn,
　His head wet with the dew.

4 Love thou the path thy Saviour trod,
　And patient wait thy rest;
His holy city thou shalt see,
　Home of the loved and blest!
　　　　Sarah Roberts Boyle, 1853. Ab. and alt.

THE RESURRECTION.

241 ROLL CALL.

JAMES MILTON BLACK, 1893.

THE HOMELAND.

yon - der, When the roll is called up yon - der, I'll be there.

2 On that bright and cloudless morning when the dead in Christ shall rise,
   And the glory of His resurrection share;
  When His chosen ones shall gather to their home beyond the skies,
   And the roll is called up yonder, I'll be there.

3 Let us labor for the Master from the dawn till setting sun,
   Let us talk of all His wondrous love and care,
  Then when all of life is over and our work on earth is done,
   And the roll is called up yonder, I'll be there.
                                      James Milton Black, 1893.

242   HOMELAND. 7. 6. D.   ARTHUR SEYMOUR SULLIVAN, 1867.

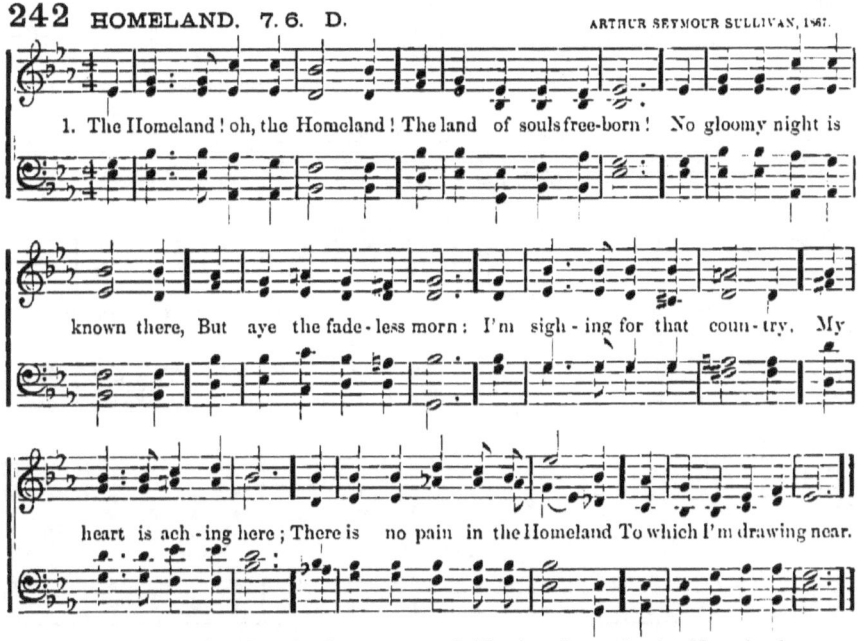

1. The Homeland! oh, the Homeland! The land of souls free-born! No gloomy night is known there, But aye the fade-less morn: I'm sigh-ing for that coun-try, My heart is ach-ing here; There is no pain in the Homeland To which I'm drawing near.

2 My Lord is in the Homeland,
   With angels bright and fair;
  No sinful thing nor evil
   Can ever enter there;
  The music of the ransomed
   Is ringing in my ears,
  And when I think of the Homeland,
   My eyes are wet with tears.

3 For loved ones in the Homeland
   Are waiting me to come
  Where neither death nor sorrow
   Invade their holy home:
  O dear, dear native Country!
   O rest and peace above!
  Christ bring us all to the Homeland
   Of His eternal love.
                Rev. Hugh Reginald Haweis, 1855.

THE ANGELS' SONG.

243 VOX ANGELICA. 11.10. With Refrain. Rev. JOHN BACCHUS DYKES, 1868.

2 Onward we go, for still we hear them singing,
   "Come, weary souls! for Jesus bids you come!"
   And through the dark its echoes sweetly ringing,
   The music of the gospel leads us home.

3 Far, far away, like bells at evening pealing,
   The voice of Jesus sounds o'er land and sea;
   And laden souls, by thousands meekly stealing,
   Kind Shepherd! turn their weary steps to Thee.

LONGING FOR HOME.

4 Rest comes at length; though life be long and dreary,
  The day must dawn, and darksome night be past;
  Faith's journey ends in welcome to the weary,
  And Heaven, the heart's true home, will come at last.

5 Angels! sing on: your faithful watches keeping,
  Sing us sweet fragments of the songs above;
  Till morning's joy shall end the night of weeping,
  And life's long shadows break in cloudless love.

Rev. Frederick William Faber, 1854. Ab. and v. 4 alt.

244 PARADISE. C. M. With Refrain.   JOSEPH BARNBY, 1866.

1. O Par - a - dise! O Par - a - dise! Who doth not crave for rest?
Who would not seek the hap - py land Where they that lov'd are blest?

Refrain.
Where loy - al hearts and true Stand ev - er in the light,
All rap - ture thro' and through, In God's most ho - ly sight?

2 O Paradise! O Paradise!
  The world is growing old;
  Who would not be at rest and free
  Where love is never cold.

3 O Paradise! O Paradise!
  I want to sin no more,
  I want to be as pure on earth
  As on thy spotless shore.

4 O Paradise! O Paradise!
  I greatly long to see
  The special place my dearest Lord
  In love prepares for me.

5 Lord Jesus, King of Paradise,
  O keep me in Thy love,
  And guide me to that happy land
  Of perfect rest above.

Rev. Frederick William Faber, 1862, 1868. Ab. and alt.

2 Those bulwarks of jasper all glorious gleam;
  Those portals of pearl stand awide;
And clear as a current of crystal the stream,
  Where branches of healing divide.
No burden of care we have carried of old,
  Those beautiful gates shall pass through;
But sweetly we'll rest in the City of Gold,
  The City where all is made new.

BEYOND THE STARS.

3 O Throne of the Thorn-crowned, ineffable, bright,
　　Where kings cast their crowns and adore!
　O Temple of God, where the Lamb is the light,
　　Where darkness and pain come no more!
　Rejoice all ye fearful, He bids you be bold;
　　His promise is spoken to you;
　His welcome awaits in the City of Gold,
　　The City where all is made new.

4 Rejoice, be not troubled; He went to prepare
　　That blessed and beautiful home,
　Which all who have loved Him forever shall share;
　　Where naught that defileth shall come.
　Oh, were it not so He would surely have told,
　　His sayings are faithful and true;
　He waits at the gates of the City of Gold,
　　The City where all is made new.
　　　　　　　　　　　　Emma Smuller Carter, 1894.

246 VESPER. 8.7.

FRIEDRICH FREIHERR von FLOTOW, 1847.
Arr. by C. ARTHUR JACQUES, 1885.

1. This is not my place of resting; Mine's a city yet to come;
Onward to it I am hasting, On to my eternal home.

2 In it all is light and glory;
　O'er it shines a nightless day:
Every trace of sin's sad story,
　All the curse, hath passed away.

3 There the Lamb, our Shepherd, leads us
　By the streams of life along,—
On the freshest pastures feeds us,
　Turns our sighing into song.

4 Soon we pass this desert dreary,
　Soon we bid farewell to pain;
Never more are sad or weary,
　Never, never sin again!
　　　　　　Rev. Horatius Bonar, 1845.

2 In the midst of that dear City
　Christ is reigning on His seat,
And the angels swing their censers
　In a ring about His feet.

3 From the throne a river issues,
　Clear as crystal, passing bright,
And it traverses the City
　Like a sudden beam of light.

4 There the wind is sweetly fragrant,
　And is laden with the song
Of the seraphs, and the elders,
　And the great redeemed throng.

5 Oh, I would my ears were open
　Here to catch that happy strain!
Oh, I would my eyes some vision
　Of that Eden could attain!
　　　　　Rev. Sabine Baring-Gould, 1865. Ab.

247

1 Daily, daily sing the praises
　Of the City God hath made;
In the beauteous fields of Eden
　Its foundation-stones are laid.

THE CELESTIAL COUNTRY.

248 GLADNESS. 7. 6. D. JOSEPH BARNBY, 1868.

1. For thee, O dear, dear Country, Mine eyes their vigils keep; For very love, beholding Thy happy name, they weep. The mention of thy glory Is unction to the breast, And medicine in sickness, And love, and life, and rest.

2 With jasper glow thy bulwarks,
   Thy streets with emeralds blaze;
The sardius and the topaz
   Unite in thee their rays;
Thy ageless walls are bonded
   With amethyst unpriced;
Thy saints build up the fabric,
   The corner-stone is CHRIST!

3 Thou hast no shore, fair ocean;
   Thou hast no time, bright day:
Dear fountain of refreshment
   To pilgrims far away.
Upon the Rock of Ages
   They raise thy holy tower;
Thine is the victor's laurel,
   And thine the golden dower.

4 And there is David's fountain,
   And life in fullest glow;
And there the light is golden,
   And milk and honey flow;
The light that hath no evening,
   The health that hath no sore,
The life that hath no ending,
   But lasteth evermore.

               Bernard of Cluny, c. 1145.
Tr. by Rev. John Mason Neale, 1851. Ab. and sl. alt.

249

1 Jerusalem, the glorious!
   The glory of the elect!
O dear and future vision
   That eager hearts expect!
Even now by faith I see thee,
   Even here thy walls discern;
To thee my thoughts are kindled,
   And strive, and pant, and yearn!

2 There Jesus shall embrace us,
   There Jesus be embraced,—
That spirit's food and sunshine,
   Whence earthly love is chased:
Then all the halls of Zion
   For aye shall be complete,
And in that land of beauty,
   All things of beauty meet.

3 The Cross is all thy splendor,
   The Crucified, thy praise;
His laud and benediction
   Thy ransomed people raise;—
Jerusalem! exulting
   On that securest shore,
I hope thee, wish thee, sing thee,
   And love thee evermore!

               Bernard of Cluny, c. 1145.
Tr. by Rev. John Mason Neale, 1851. Ab.

THE CITY OF GOD.

250 EWING. 7. 6. D. ALEXANDER EWING, 1853.

1. Jerusalem, the golden, With milk and honey blest, Beneath thy contemplation Sink heart and voice oppressed: I know not, oh, I know not, What social joys are there; What radiancy of glory, What light beyond compare.

2 They stand, those halls of Zion,
  Conjubilant with song,
And bright with many an angel,
  And all the martyr throng:
The Prince is ever in them,
  The daylight is serene;
The pastures of the blessèd
  Are decked in glorious sheen.

3 There is the throne of David;
  And there, from care released,
The shout of them that triumph,
  The song of them that feast;
And they who, with their Leader,
  Have conquered in the fight,
Forever, and forever,
  Are clad in robes of white.
      Bernard of Cluny, c. 1145.
      Tr. by Rev. John Mason Neale, 1851. Ab.

2 And now we fight the battle,
  But then shall wear the crown
Of full, and everlasting,
  And passionless renown.
But He whom now we trust in
  Shall then be seen and known;
And they that know and see Him
  Shall have Him for their own.

3 The morning shall awaken,
  The shadows shall decay,
And each true-hearted servant
  Shall shine as doth the day.
There God our King and Portion,
  In fulness of His grace,
We then shall see forever,
  And worship face to face.
      Bernard of Cluny, c. 1145.
      Tr. by Rev. John Mason Neale, 1851. Ab. and alt.

251

1 Brief life is here our portion;
  Brief sorrow, short-lived care;
The life that knows no ending,
  The tearless life, is there.
O happy retribution:
  Short toil, eternal rest;
For mortals and for sinners
  A mansion with the blest.

252

1 O sweet and blessèd Country!
  Shall I e'er see thy face?
O sweet and blessèd Country!
  Shall I e'er win thy grace?—
Jesus in mercy bring us
  To that dear land of rest,
Who art with God the Father,
  And Spirit ever blest.
      Bernard of Cluny, c. 1145.
      Tr. by Rev. John Mason Neale, 1851.

LONGING FOR HOME.

253 CASTLE RISING. C. M. D.
Rev. FREDERICK ALFRED JOHN HERVEY, 1-6:.

1. The roseate hues of early dawn,
The brightness of the day,
The crimson of the sunset sky,
How fast they fade away!
Oh, for the pearly gates of Heav'n!
Oh, for the golden floor!
Oh, for the Sun of Righteousness,
That setteth nevermore!

2 The highest hopes we cherish here,
How soon they tire and faint!
How many a spot defiles the robe
That wraps an earthly saint!
Oh, for a heart that never sins!
Oh, for a soul washed white!
Oh, for a voice to praise our King,
Nor weary day nor night!

3 Here faith is ours, and heavenly hope,
And grace to lead us higher;
But there are perfectness and peace,
Beyond our best desire.
Oh, by Thy love and anguish, Lord,
And by Thy life laid down,
Grant that we fail not of Thy grace,
Nor cast away our crown!

Cecil Frances Alexander, 1852. Sl. alt.

254 (DUKE STREET). L. M.

1 O God, beneath Thy guiding hand,
Our exiled fathers crossed the sea;
And when they trod the wintry strand,
With prayer and psalm they worshiped Thee.

2 Thou heard'st, well-pleased, the song, the prayer;
Thy blessing came; and still its power
Shall onward through all ages bear
The memory of that holy hour.

3 Laws, freedom, truth, and faith in God
Came with those exiles o'er the waves;
And where their pilgrim feet have trod,
The God they trusted guards their graves.

4 And here Thy Name, O God of love,
Their children's children shall adore,
Till these eternal hills remove,
And spring adorns the earth no more.

Rev. Leonard Bacon, 1833, 1845.

GOD IN NATURE.

255 RYMER'S TOWER.
Rev. JAMES CARTER, 1898.

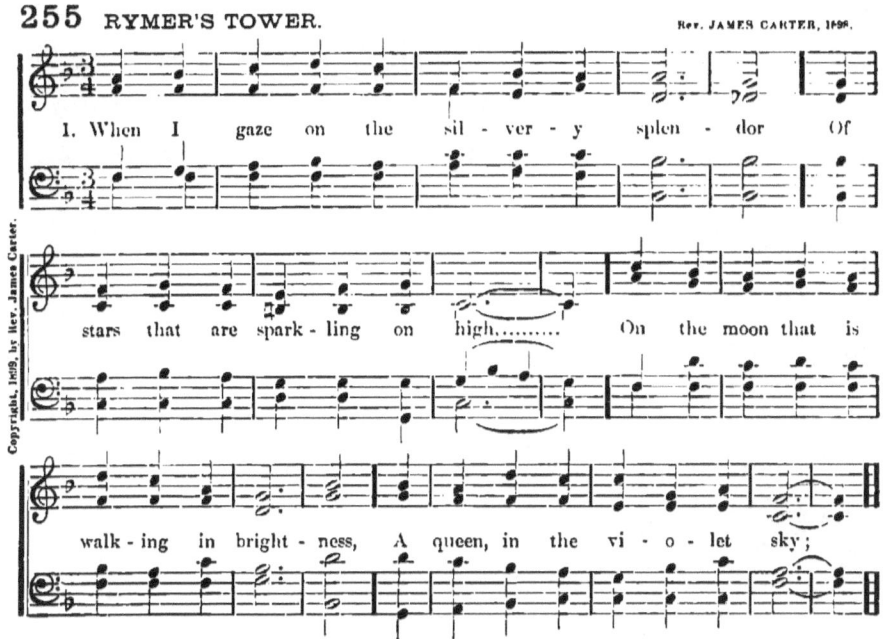

1. When I gaze on the sil-ver-y splen-dor Of stars that are spark-ling on high,........ On the moon that is walk-ing in bright-ness, A queen, in the vi-o-let sky;

2 What is man that Thou thinkest upon him,
   Great God, the Creator of light?
   That Thou makest him next to the angels
   And givest him honor and might?

3 For Thou crownest the year with Thy goodness;
   With mercy Thou fillest our days.
   Oh, forbid that we e'er should forget Thee,
   Or weary of singing Thy praise.
   Agnes Carter Mason, 1883.

DUKE STREET. L. M.
JOHN HATTON, c. 1790.

1. O God, be-neath Thy guid-ing hand, Our ex-iled fa-thers crossed the sea; And when they trod the win-try strand, With pray'r and psalm they worshiped Thee.

THE JOY OF HARVEST.

256 HARVEST HOME. Rev. JAMES CARTER, 1896.

1. After the heat of the summer sun,
   After the harvest days are done,
   After the golden sheaves are won,
   Rest in the harvest home.
   Harvest home! Harvest home!
   (Rest)
   (Joy) in the harvest, harvest home
   (Peace)
   (Rest)
   (Joy) in the harvest, harvest home,
   (Peace)
   home, home.
   Oh, 'twill be sweet to find at last
   (Rest)
   (Joy) in the harvest home.
   (Peace)

2 After the falterings and the fears,
  After the trials and the tears,
  After the waiting of weary years
  Joy in the harvest home.

3 After the trouble and toil are past,
  After the striving, fierce and fast,
  Oh, 'twill be sweet to find at last
  Peace in the harvest home.
  Emma Smuller Carter, 1896.

257 (ST. GEORGE'S CHAPEL). 7. D.

1 Thou who roll'st the year around,
    Crowned with mercies large and free,
  Rich Thy gifts to us abound,
    Warm our thanks shall rise to Thee:
  Kindly to our worship bow,
    While our grateful praises swell,
  That, sustained by Thee, we now
    Bid the parting year farewell.

2 All its numbered days are sped,
    All its busy scenes are o'er,
  All its joys for ever fled,
    All its sorrows felt no more:

  Mingled with th' eternal past,
    Its remembrance shall decay;
  Yet to be revived at last
    At the solemn judgment-day.

3 All our follies, Lord, forgive;
    Cleanse each heart and make us Thine;
  Let Thy grace within us live,
    As our future suns decline;
  Then, when life's last eve shall come,
    Happy spirits, let us fly
  To our everlasting home,
    To our Father's house **on high.**
    Rev. Ray Palmer, 1832.

THANKSGIVING.

258 ST. GEORGE'S CHAPEL. 7. D. Sir GEORGE JOB ELVEY. 1852.

1. Come, ye thankful people, come,
Raise the song of Harvest-home:
All is safely gather'd in,
Ere the winter storms begin;
God, our Maker, doth provide
For our wants to be supplied:
Come to God's own temple, come,
Raise the song of Harvest-home.

2 All the world is God's own field,
Fruit unto His praise to yield;
Wheat and tares together sown,
Unto joy or sorrow grown;
First the blade, and then the ear,
Then the full corn shall appear:
Lord of Harvest, grant that we
Wholesome grain and pure may be.

3 For the Lord our God shall come,
And shall take His harvest home;
From His field shall in that day
All offences purge away;
Give His angels charge at last
In the fire the tares to cast;
But the fruitful ears to store
In His garner evermore.

4 Even so, Lord, quickly come
To Thy final Harvest home;
Gather Thou Thy people in,
Free from sorrow, free from sin;
There, forever purified,
In Thy presence to abide:
Come, with all Thine angels, come,
Raise the glorious Harvest-home.

Rev. Henry Alford, 1844.

OUR COUNTRY AND THE WORLD.

259 AMERICA. 6. 6. 4. 6. 6. 6. 4.   HENRY CAREY, 1740. Har. 1745.

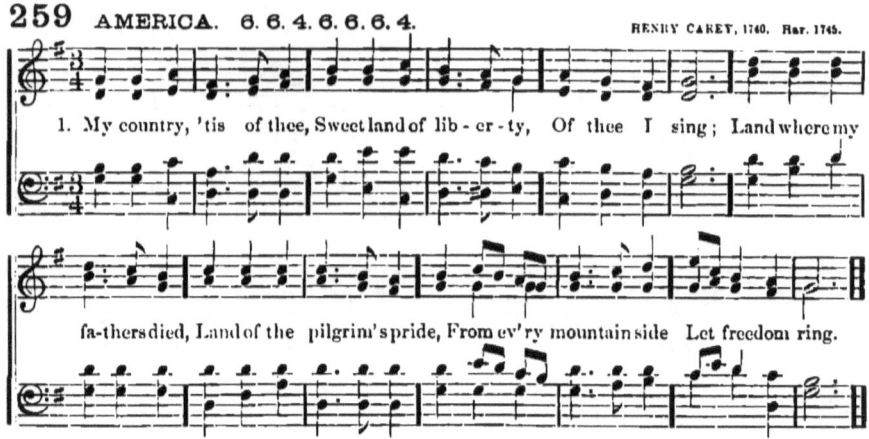

1. My country, 'tis of thee, Sweet land of lib-er-ty, Of thee I sing; Land where my fa-thers died, Land of the pilgrim's pride, From ev'ry mountain side Let freedom ring.

2 My native country, thee,
Land of the noble, free,
  Thy name I love;
I love thy rocks and rills,
Thy woods and templed hills;
My heart with rapture thrills
  Like that above.

3 Let music swell the breeze,
And ring from all the trees
  Sweet freedom's song:
Let mortal tongues awake,
Let all that breathe partake,
Let rocks their silence break,
  The sound prolong.

4 Our father's God, to Thee,
Author of liberty,
  To Thee we sing;
Long may our land be bright
With freedom's holy light;
Protect us by Thy might,
  Great God, our King.
Rev. Samuel Francis Smith, 1832.

260

1 God bless our native land:
Firm may she ever stand,
  Through storm and night;
When the wild tempests rave,
Ruler of wind and wave,
Do Thou our country save
  By Thy great might.

2 For her our prayer shall rise
To God, above the skies;
  On Him we wait;

Thou who art ever nigh,
Guarding with watchful eye,
  To Thee aloud we cry,
  God save the State.
Rev. Charles Timothy Brooks, 1835.
Alt. by Rev. John Sullivan Dwight, 1844.

261

1 Christ for the world we sing;
The world to Christ we bring,
  With loving zeal;
The poor, and them that mourn,
The faint and overborne,
Sin-sick and sorrow-worn,
  Whom Christ doth heal.

2 Christ for the world we sing;
The world to Christ we bring,
  With fervent prayer;
The wayward and the lost,
By restless passions tossed,
Redeemed at countless cost
  From dark despair.

3 Christ for the world we sing;
The world to Christ we bring,
  With one accord;
With us the work to share,
With us reproach to dare,
With us the cross to bear,
  For Christ our Lord.

4 Christ for the world we sing;
The world to Christ we bring,
  With joyful song;
The new-born souls, whose days,
Reclaimed from error's ways,
Inspired with hope and praise,
  To Christ belong.
Rev. Samuel Wolcott, 1869.

THE BATTLE HYMN OF THE REPUBLIC.

262 REPUBLIC. Arr. by C. ARTHUR JACQUES, 1898. Popular Air.

1. Mine eyes have seen the glory of the coming of the Lord, He is trampling out the vintage where the grapes of wrath are stored! He hath loosed the fateful lightning of His terrible swift sword; His truth is marching on.

Chorus.
Glory, glory, hallelujah! Glory, glory, hallelujah! Glory, glory, hallelujah! Our God is marching on.

2 He has sounded forth the trumpet that shall never call retreat;
He is sifting out the hearts of men before His judgment-seat;
Oh, be swift, my soul, to answer Him! be jubilant, my feet!
　　Our God is marching on.

3 In the beauty of the lilies Christ was born across the sea,
With a glory in His bosom that transfigures you and me:
As He died to make men holy, let us die to make men free,
　　While God is marching on.
　　　　　　Mrs. Julia Ward Howe, 1861.

ALPHABETICAL INDEX OF TUNES.

All Saints..................175	Ensign......................207	Laban......................179	Roll Call....................241
Almsgiving..........26, 111	Entreaty...................101	Labarum..................194	Rubinstein................155
America....................239	Er Sorget..................140	Laud..........................36	Russia........................60
Amicus.....................141	Ercildoun.................120	Lambeth..................144	Rymer's Tower........255
Angelus. (L. M.) 12, 198	Erie............................27	Lead Me, Saviour....173	
Angelus. (P. M.).......7	Eshtemon............136, 231	Leominster..............239	St. Agnes........125, 148, 205
Antioch......................46	Eucharist.................228	Livorno....................164	St. Alphege........213, 227
Arcadelt......................6	Evan........................142	Lorelei.....................138	St. Ann's..........150, 218
Ariel.........................126	Evelyn.......................92	Louvan......................31	St. George's Chapel...258
Arlington..........146, 186	Eventide....................18	Lux Benigna............162	St. Helen's...............110
Aspiration................130	Ewing......................230	Lyons........................40	St. Hilda..................115
Athens.......................72			St. Mark....................54
Augusta....................91	Falfield...................216	Maitland..................188	Seymour.....................5
Aurelia...............37, 225	Federal Street.........121	Manoah.....................33	Siloam.....................221
Autumn.....................65	Flemming................149	Martyn................78, 180	Smuller...................245
Avon....................50, 55	Fons Salutis..............85	Merrial......................11	State Street........79, 214
Azmon.................59, 220		Messiah...................211	Stephanos.................97
	Galilee....................109	Missionary Chant....237	Stephens....................63
Barnegat..................28	Germany...................52	Missionary Hymn....233	Stowe......................127
Bartimaeus.............170	Gertrude.................163	Mozart......................57	Stockwell................202
Basel.......................222	Gladness............235, 248		Submission..............112
Beatitude................223	Glory..........................4	Navigans...................95	Supplication............116
Berlin......................168	God be with you.......17	Nettleton...................35	Sunshine.................196
Bethany. (6. 4.).......133		Nicaea........................1	
Bethany. (8. 7. D.)...74	Halle...........................9		Temptation.............183
Bethel......................132	Hamburg...................56	O Agne Dei...............53	Thatcher..................143
Bethlehem.................44	Hammer...................182	Old Hundred.............39	To-day......................82
Bon Cœur................174	Harvest Home.........256	Olivet......................110	Toplady...................113
Boylston..............77, 181	Haydn........................64	Only a Step...............84	Trusting..................100
Bradford....................62	Heber......................123	Oriens.........................3	
	Hebron......................14	Ortonville................122	Uxbridge...................29
Calvary................48, 153	Hendon...............137, 172	Ossining....................90	
Carol..........................42	Hither.......................96		Venio.......................117
Carter........................34	Hodnet....................165	Palmer.....................105	Vesper.....................246
Castle Rising..........253	Hollingside.............180	Paradise..................244	Vesperalis.................15
Chesterfield........30, 128	Holy Cross...............240	Park Street..............176	Victory......................61
Christmas'...........43, 185	Home......................210	Passion Chorale......226	Vigilate...................184
Conflict...................200	Homeland...............242	Pax Tecum..............135	Vineyard.................193
Conrad......................22	Hora Occidua............16	Penitence................114	Vox Angelica..........243
Coronation................41	Horeb........................69	Pentecost..................68	Vox Clamantis........192
Cowper......................73	Horton.......................24	Petition.....................70	
	Hudson......................4	Pilot.........................171	Walter.....................160
Dedham..................219	Hursley.....................20	Portuguese Hymn....139	Wanderer..................86
Dedication...............157		Proclamation..........195	Warfare....................94
Dennis....................215	Ignatius....................21		Webb.......................190
Dix......................47, 161	I love to tell the story 75	Quebec....................190	Whitaker..........103, 224
Dorrnance.................99	Invitation..................88		Whosoever................83
Duke Street...178, 203, 254	Italian Hymn..............2	Rathbun..................147	Wiltwyck.................134
Dundee......................32		Regent Square........166	Wimborne................206
	Jesus I Come...........102	Renovation........187, 208	Wondrous Love........76
Earlstoun................197	Jesus Mihi Moritur...118	Retreat......................23	Woodworth..............107
Easter Morning.........58	Jewett.....................151	Robinson............19, 158	
Ellerton.....................25		Rockingham..............51	Zephyr....................229
Endeavor................212	Kenosis.....................45		

METRICAL INDEX OF TUNES.

C. M.

Antioch...46
Arlington...146, 186
Avon...50, 55
Azmon...59, 220
Beatitude...223
Bradford...62
Calvary...48, 153
Chesterfield...30, 128
Christmas...43, 185
Coronation...41
Cowper...73
Dedham...219
Dundee...32
Evan...142
Heber...123
Horeb...69
Holy Cross...240
Laud...36
Lambeth...141
Maitland...188
Manoah...33
Ortonville...122
Paradise...244
Pentecost...68
St. Agnes...125, 148, 205
St. Ann's...150, 218
St. Mark...54
Siloam...221
Stephens...63
Wondrous Love...76

C. M. D.

All Saints...175
Aspiration...130
Athens...72
Bon Cœur...174
Carol...42
Castle Rising...253
Hamner...182

L. M.

Angelus...12, 198
Duke Street...178, 203, 254
Ensign...207
Evelyn...92
Federal Street...121
Germany...52
Hamburg...56
Hebron...14
Hursley...20
Louvan...31
Missionary Chant...237
Old Hundred...39
Park Street...176
Quebec...199
Retreat...23
Rockingham...51
Uxbridge...29
Woodworth...107
Zephyr...229

L. M. D.

O Agne Dei...53

S. M.

Arcadelt...6
Boylston...77, 181
Dennis...215
Glory...4
Haydn...64
Hudson...4
Ignatius...21
Laban...179
Labarum...194
Renovation...187, 208
State Street...79, 214
Thatcher...143

S. M. D.

Leominster...230

C. P. M.

Ariel...126

5. 4. 5. 4.

Venio...117

5. 4. 5. 4. D.

Amicus...141

6. D.

Jewett...151

6. 4.

To-day...82

6. 4. 6. 4.
6. 6. 6. 4.

Bethany...133
Bethel...132
Robinson...19, 158

6. 6. 4. 6. 6. 6. 4.

America...250
Italian Hymn...2
Olivet...119

6. 5.

Hora Occidua...16
Merrial...11

6. 5. 12 lines.

Gertrude...163
Proclamation...195

7.

Berlin...168
Eshtemoa...136, 231
Hendon...137, 172
Horton...24
Lead Me, Saviour...173
Livorno...164
Mozart...57
Rubinstein...155
Seymour...5
Trusting...109
Wanderer...86

7. 6 lines.

Dix...47, 161
Halle...9
Penitence...114
Pilot...171
Submission...112
Toplady...113

7. D.

Hollingside...180
Martyn...78, 180
Messiah...211
St. George's Chapel...258

7. 3. 7. 7. 7. 3.

Walter...160

7. 6.

St. Alphege...213, 227

7. 6. D.

Aurelia...37, 252
Ewing...250
Fons Salutis...85
Gladness...235, 248
Hither...96
Hodnet...165
Homeland...242
I love to tell the...75
Missionary Hymn...233
Ossining...90
Passion Chorale...226
St. Hilda...115
Webb...190
Whosoever...83

7. 7. 4. 7. 7. 4.

Er Sorget...140

7. 7. 7. 3.

Vigilate...184

8. 5. 8. 3.

St. Helen's...110
Stephanos...97

8. 6. 8. 5.

Navigans...95

8. 7.

Bartimaeus...170
Carter...34
Dorrnance...99
Ercildoun...120
Rathbun...147
Russia...60
Stockwell...202
Vesper...246

8. 7. D.

Autumn...65
Bethany...74
Earlstoun...197
Endeavor...212
Erie...27

Falfield...216
Nettleton...35
Oriens...3
Warfare...91
Whitaker...103, 224

8. 7. 4.

Regent Square...166
Victory...61

8. 7. 8. 7. 7. 7.

Bethlehem...44

8. 7. 8. 8. 8. 7.

Dedication...157

8. 8. 8. 4.

Almsgiving...26, 111
Conrad...22

8. 8. 8. 6.

Flemming...149

8. 8. 8. 7. D.

Conflict...200
Home...210

9. 8.

Petition...70
Vesperalis...15
Wimborne...206

10. 2 lines.

Pax Tecum...135

10.

Ellerton...25
Eventide...18

10. 4. 0. 10.

Lux Benigna...162

10. 8.

Rymer's Tower...255

10. 11.

Lyons...40

11.

Portuguese Hymn...139

11. 10.

Smuller...245

11. 8.

Eucharist...228
Stowe...127
Vox Angelica...243

11. 10. 11. 4.

Wiltwyck...134

12. 11.

Barnegat...28

INDEX

OF

AUTHORS AND TRANSLATORS.

ADAMS, Sarah Flower (Mrs. W. B.) (1805-1848), 132.
Alexander, Cecil Frances (Mrs. W.) (1823-1895), 99, 253.
Alexander, Rev. James Waddell, D. D. (1804-1859), 226.
Alford, Rev. Henry, D. D. (1810-1871), 258.
Allen, Rev. James (1734-1804), 224.
BACON, Rev. Leonard, D. D. (1802-1881), 254.
Baker, Miss Mary A. (   ), 169.
Baring-Gould, Rev. Sabine (1834—), 11, 163, 217, 247.
Beddome, Rev. Benjamin (1717-1795), 29.
Beecher, Rev. Charles (1819—), 188.
Bernard of Cluny (11th Century), 248, 249, 250, 251, 252.
Bernard of Clairvaux (1091-1153), 125, 226.
Bickersteth, Bp. Edward Henry, D. D. (1825—), 37, 135.
Black, James Milton (   ), 241.
Bonar, Rev. Horatius, D. D. (1808-1889), 44, 72, 152, 198, 201, 246.
Borthwick, Miss Jane (1813—), 151.
Bowring, Sir John (1792-1872), 34, 147.
Boyle, Sarah Roberts (Mrs.) (1812-1869), 240.
Brady, Rev. Nicholas, D. D. (1659-1726), 36.
Bridges, Matthew (1800-?), 124.
Brooks, Rev. Charles Timothy (1813-1883), 260.
Brown, Phœbe Hinsdale (Mrs. T. H.) (1783-1861), 67.
Burgess, Bp. George, D. D. (1829-1866), 209.
Burns, Rev. James Drummond (1823-1864), 6.
CARTER, Emma Smuller (Mrs. James), 3, 68, 84, 88, 89, 101, 112, 116, 118, 130, 140, 157, 160, 164, 192, 194, 197, 222, 245, 256.
Carter, Rev. James, 16, 19, 28, 45, 53, 58, 70, 71, 83, 85, 90, 91, 92, 94, 95, 96, 114, 117, 134, 174, 193, 195, 196, 200, 206, 210, 212, 213, 228, 235.
Cary, Miss Phœbe (1824-1871), 239.

Caswall, Rev. Edward (1814-1878), 125.
Cennick, Rev. John (1718-1755), 172.
Clark, Rev. James Freeman, D. D. (1810-1888), 86.
Conder, Josiah (1789-1855), 52.
Cotterill, Rev. Thomas (1779-1823), 29.
Cousin, Anne Ross (Mrs W.) (   ), 120.
Coxe, Bp. Arthur Cleveland (1818-1896), 218.
Cowper, William (1731-1800), 30, 73, 145, 150, 191.
Crewdson, Jane (Mrs. F.) (1809-1863), 153.
DAVIES, Rev. Samuel (1723-1761), 229.
Davis, Frank M. (   ), 173.
Deck, James George (1802-1884), 225.
Dix, William Chatterton (1837—), 47, 54.
Doane, Bp. George Washington, D. D. (1799-1859), 5, 49, 207.
Dobell, John (1737-1840), 80.
Doddridge, Rev. Philip, D. D. (1702-1751), 185, 220.
Duffield, Rev. George, D. D. (1818-1888), 190.
Dwight, Rev. John Sullivan (1813—), 214.
Dwight, Rev. Timothy, D. D. (1752-1817), 214.
EDMESTON, James (1791-1867), 167.
Ellerton, Rev. John (1826-1893), 15, 21, 25.
Elliott, Miss Charlotte (1789-1873), 26, 107, 111, 149, 184.
English Author, 205.
Everest, Rev. Charles William (1814-1877), 203.
FABER, Rev. Frederick William, D. D. (1814-1863), 33, 74, 128, 243, 244.
Fawcett, Rev. John, D. D. (1740-1817), 215.
Findlater, Sarah (Mrs. E. J.) (1823—), 108.
Francis, Rev. Benjamin (1734-1799), 121.
GERHARDT, Rev. Paul (1607-1641), 226.
Gould, see Baring-Gould.
Grant, Sir Robert (1785-1838), 40.
Griggs, Rev. Joseph (c. 1720-1768), 121.
Gurney, Rev. John Hampden (1802-1862), 50.

HANKEY, Miss Katherine ( ), 75.
Hart, Rev. Joseph (1712-1768), 64.
Hastings, Thomas, Mus. Doc. (1786-1872). 10, 82, 202.
Havergal, Miss Frances Ridley (1836-1879), 110, 170, 198, 211, 227.
Haweis, Rev. Hugh Reginald (1838—), 242.
Heath, Rev. George (?-1822), 179.
Heber, Bp. Reginald, D. D. (1783-1826), 1, 175, 221, 233.
Holmes, Oliver Wendell, M. D., LL.D. (1809-1894), 31.
Hopper, Rev. Edward, D. D. (1818-1888), 171.
How, Bp. William Walsham, D. D. (1823—), 38, 115, 161, 208.
INGEMANN, Bernhardt Severin (1789-1862), 217.
KEBLE, Rev. John (1792-1866), 20.
Keen, 139.
Kelly, Rev. Thomas (1769-1855), 59, 61, 136, 187.
Kennedy, Rev. Benjamin Hall, D. D. (1804-1889), 137.
LEESON, Miss Jane E. (19th Century), 168.
Logan, Rev. John (1748-1788), 220.
Lyte, Rev. Henry Francis (1793-1847), 18, 103.
McDONALD, Rev. William (1820—), 109.
Mason, Agnes Carter (Mrs. Frank G.), 255.
Maude, Mary Fawler (Mrs. J.), (1819—), 231.
Medley, Rev. Samuel (1738-1799), 126.
Monsell, Rev. John Samuel Bewley, LL.D. (1811-1875), 141, 177.
Montgomery, James (1771-1854), 66, 223, 232, 234, 238.
Morgan, Rev. S. C. ( ), 98.
Muhlenberg, Rev. William Augustus, D. D. (1796-1877), 81.
NEALE, Rev. John Mason, D. D. (1818-1866), 8, 97, 248, 249, 250, 251, 252.
Newton, Rev. John (1725-1807), 24, 123, 216.
Newman, Rev. John Henry, D. D. (1801-1890), 162.
ONDERDONK, Bp. Henry Ustick, D. D. (1779-1858), 79.
PALMER, Horatio Richmond, Mus. Doc. (1834—), 183.
Palmer, Rev. Ray, D. D. (1808-1887), 104, 119, 148, 257.
Patrick, Bp. John, D. D. (17th Century), 36.
Perronet, Rev. Edward (1726-1795), 41.
Prentiss, Elizabeth Payson, (Mrs. G. L.) (1818-1878), 133.

RANKIN, Rev. Jeremiah Eames, D. D. (1828—), 7, 17, 100, 102.
Rawson, George (1807-1889), 155, 156.
Raymond, Rossiter Worthington (1840—), 138.
Reed, Eliza Holmes (Mrs. Andrew) (1794-1867), 93.
Reed, Rev. Andrew, D. D. (1787-1862), 69.
Rippon, Rev. John, D. D. (1751-1836), 41.
Robinson, Rev. Charles Seymour, D. D. (1829-1899), 158.
Robinson, Rev. Robert (1735-1790), 35.
Rous, Francis (1579-1659), 142.
SCHMOLKE, Rev. Benjamin (1672-1737), 151.
Schwedler, Rev. Johann Christoph (1672-1730), 137.
Scriven, Joseph (1829-1856), 27.
Sears, Rev. Edmund Hamilton, D. D. (1810-1879), 42.
Shirley, Rev. Walter (1725-1786), 224.
Shepherd, Rev. Thomas (1665-1739), 188.
Sleight, Miss Mary B. ( ), 105.
Smith, Rev. Samuel Francis, D. D. (1808-1895), 82, 236, 259.
Stennett, Rev. Samuel, D. D. (1727-1795), 122.
Stockton, Martha Matilda (Mrs. W. C.) (1821-1885), 76.
Stowell, Rev. Hugh (1799-1865), 23.
Stephen of St. Sabas (725-797), 97.
Swain, Rev. Leonard, D. D. (1821-1869), 180.
TATE, Nahum (1652-1715), 36, 43.
Taylor, Rev. Thomas Rawson (1807-1835), 159.
Tersteegen, Rev. Gerhard (1697-1769), 108.
Thring, Rev. Godfrey (1823—), 22.
Toplady, Rev. Augustus Montague (1740-1778), 113.
Tuttiett, Rev. Lawrence (1825—), 182.
Twells, Rev. Henry (1823—), 12.
UNKNOWN Author, 2, 36, 60, 87, 106, 127, 154.
WARING, Miss Anna Laetitia (1820—), 165.
Watts, Rev. Isaac, D. D. (1674-1748), 4, 13, 14, 32, 39, 46, 51, 55, 56, 63, 77, 143, 146, 176, 178, 186, 204, 237.
Wesley, Rev. Charles (1707-1788), 9, 57, 62, 65, 78, 129, 131, 144, 181, 189, 219.
Wesley, Rev. John (1703-1791), 39.
Whittier, John Greenleaf (1807-1892), 48.
Williams, Rev. Peter (1722-1796), 166.
Williams, Rev. William (1717-1791), 166.
Wolcott, Rev. Samuel, D. D. (1813-1886), 261.
Wolfe, Rev. Aaron Robarts (1821—), 230.
Woodford, Bp. James Russell, D. D. (1820-1885), 60.

INDEX

OF

COMPOSERS AND HARMONIZERS.

ALLEN, George Nelson (1812-1877), 188.
Arcadelt, Jacques (16th Century), 6.
Arne, Thomas Augustine, Mus. Doc. (1710-1778), 146 (186).

BACH, Johann Sebastian (1685-1750), 226.
Baker, Rev. Sir Henry William (1821-1877), 97, 199.
Barnby, Sir Joseph (1838-1896), 11, 235 (248), 244.
Barrows, O. R. (   ), 102.
Bartolemon, Francois Hippolite (1741-1808), 65.
Beadle, Harry Hobart (1828—), 61.
Beethoven, Ludwig von (1770-1827), 52.
Bishop, Sir Henry Rowley (1780-1855), 210.
Black, James Milton (   ), 241.
Bourgeois, Louis (1500?-1560?), 39.
Bradbury, William Batchelder (1816-1868), 107, 220.

CALDBECK, Rev. G. T. (   ), 135.
Calkin, John Baptiste (1827—), 207.
Carey, Henry (1685-1743), 259.
Carter, Rev. Edmund Sardinson (1845—), 34.
Carter, Emma Smuller (Mrs. James), 112, 160.
Carter, Rev. James, 3, 15, 16, 19 (158), 22, 28, 44, 45, 53, 58, 68, 69, 70, 83, 84, 85, 86, 88, 90, 91, 92, 94, 95, 96, 101, 114, 116, 117, 118, 120, 127, 130, 132, 134, 140, 141, 157, 174, 182, 192, 193, 194, 195, 196, 197, 212, 222, 228, 245, 255, 256.
Conkey, Ithamar (1815-1867), 147.
Converse, Hon. Charles Crozat (1834—), 27.
Croft, William, Mus. Doc. (1678-1727), 150 (218).
Cutler, Henry Stephen, Mus. Doc. (1824—), 175.

DAVIS, Frank M. (   ), 173.
Dykes, Rev. John Bacchus, Mus. Doc. (1823-1876). 1, 26 (111), 36, 125 (148, 205), 162, 189, 223, 243.

ELVEY, Sir George Job, Mus. Doc. (1816-1893), 258.
Ewing, Lt.-Col. Alexander (1830-1885), 250.

FISCHER, William Gustavus (1835—), 75, 76, 109.
Flemming, Friedrich Ferdinand (1778-1813), 149.
Flotow, Friedrich Freiherr von (1812-1883), 103 (224), 246.
Freylinghausen, Rev. Johann Anastasius (1670-1739), 168.

GARDINER, William (1770-1853), 52, 219.
Gauntlett, Henry John, Mus. Doc. (1805-1876), 21, 54, 213 (227).
Giardini, Felice de (1716-1796), 2, 72.
Gläser, Carl Gotthilf (1784-1829), 59 (220).
Gould, John Edgar (1822-1875), 171.
Greatorex, Henry Wellington (1811-1858), 5, 33.

HANDEL, George Frederick (1685-1759), 43 (185), 46, 62, 143.
Harrison, Rev. Ralph (1748-1810), 4.
Hassler, Hans Leo (1564-1612), 226.
Hastings, Thomas, Mus. Doc. (1784-1872), 23, 113, 122.
Hatton, John (?-1793), 178 (203, 254).
Havergal, Rev. William Henry (1793-1870), 142.
Haweis, Rev. Thomas, M. D. (1732-1820), 30 (128).

INDEX OF COMPOSERS AND HARMONIZERS. 159

Haydn, Francis Joseph, Mus. Doc. (1732-1809), 40, 64.
Herold, Louis Joseph Ferdinand (1791-1833), 211.
Hervey, Rev. Frederick Alfred John (1846—), 253.
Holbrook, Joseph Perry (1822-1888), 151.
Holden, Oliver (1785-1844), 41.
Hopkins, Edward John, Mus. Bac. (1818—), 25.
Hummel, Johann Nepomuk (1778-1837), 187 (208).
Husband, Rev. Edward (1843—), 115.

JACQUES, C. Arthur, 6, 48 (153), 60, 103 (224), 155, 164, 200, 210, 246, 262.
Jenks, Stephen (?-1856), 170.
Jones, Rev. Darius Eliot (1815-1881), 202.
Jones, Rev. William (1726-1800), 63.
Josephi, Georg (17th Century), 12 (198).

KINGSLEY, George (1811-1884), 123, 211.
Knecht, Justin Heinrich (1752-1817), 115.
Kocher, Conrad, Ph. D. (1786-1872), 47 (161).

LWOFF, Alexis Feodorovitch (1799-1870), 60.

MALAN, Rev. Cæsar Henri Abraham (1787-1864), 137 (172).
Mallary, Rev. Raymond DeWitt, D. D. (1851—), 7.
Marsh, Simeon Butler (1798-1875), 78 (189).
Martin, George William (1828-1881), 239.
Mascagni, Pietro (1863—), 164.
Mason, Lowell, Mus. Doc. (1792-1872), 14, 29, 46, 51, 56, 59 (220), 73, 77 (181), 82, 119, 126, 133, 142, 179, 215, 233.
Mason, Timothy Battle (1801-1861), 136 (231).
Monk, William Henry, Mus. Doc. (1823-1889), 18, 20, 47 (161), 97, 184.
Mozart, Johann C. W. A. (1756-1791), 57, 126, 240.

NÄGELI, Johann Georg (1768-1836), 215.

OLIVER, Henry Kemble (1800-1885), 121.

PALMER, Horatio Richmond, Mus. Doc. (1834—), 105, 169, 183.
Portogallo, Marc Antoine (1763-1830), 139.

RITTER, Peter (1760-1846), 9, 20.
Rossini, Gioachino Antonio (1792-1868), 33, 200.
Rubenstein, Anton Gregor (1829-1894), 155.

SILCHER, Friedrich, Ph. D. (1789-1860), 138.
Simpson, Robert (1792-1832), 65.
Smart, Henry (1813-1879), 74, 166.
Spohr, Ludwig, Mus. Doc., Ph. D. (1784-1859), 48 (153).
Stewart, Robert Prescott, Mus. Doc. (1825-1894), 110.
Strattner, Georg Christoph (1650-1705), 168.
Sullivan, Sir Arthur Seymour, Mus. Doc. (1842—), 163, 216, 239, 242.

TAYLOR, Virgil Corydon (1817—), 31.
Thalberg, Sigismund (1812-1871), 165.
Tomer, William Gould (1833-1896), 17.
Tye, Christopher, Mus. Doc. (?-1572), 32.

VENUA, Frederic Marc Antoine, M. A. (1788-1872), 176.

WADE, James Clifft (1847—), 240.
Wartensee, Xavier Schnyder von (1786-1868), 24.
Webb, George James (1803-1887), 190.
Webbe, Samuel (1740-1816), 144.
Weber, Carl Marie Friedrich von (1786-1826), 5, 151.
Wesley, Samuel Sebastian, Mus. Doc. (1810-1876), 37 (225).
Whitaker, John (1776-1847), 206.
Willis, Richard Storrs (1819—), 42.
Wilson, Hugh (1764-1824), 50 (55).
Woodbury, Isaac Baker (1819-1858), 99, 221.
Woodman, Jonathan Call (1813-1894), 79 (214).
Wyeth, Rev. John (1792-1858), 35.

ZEUNER, Heinrich Christopher (1795-1857), 237.

INDEX OF SUBJECTS.

ABBA FATHER, 103, 143.
ABIDING IN CHRIST — See *Christ, Union with.*
ACCEPTANCE OF CHRIST— See *Sinners.*
ACCEPTED TIME, 80, 81, 83, 108.
ACCESS TO GOD, 6, 23, 24, 48, 111, 132.
ACTIVITY — See *Christians, Activity of,* and *Warfare.*
ADOPTION, 111, 143.
ADVENT—See *Christ.*
AFFLICTION:
  BLESSING OF, 149, 150, 153, 155, 158.
  COMFORT UNDER, 138, 139, 142, 170, 191, 243.
  COURAGE IN, 142, 153, 154, 158, 165, 186.
  DELIVERANCE FROM, 139, 169.
  PRAYER IN, 27, 119, 132, 155, 169.
  REFUGE IN, 12, 23, 139, 169, 170, 189.
  REJOICING IN, 72, 187.
  SUBMISSION UNDER, 144, 149, 151, 154, 158.
ALL IN ALL—See *Christ* and *God.*
ANGELS:
  AT THE CORONATION OF CHRIST, 41, 61.
  AT THE FIRST ADVENT OF CHRIST, 42, 43.
  AT THE RESURRECTION OF CHRIST, 57, 58.
  AT THE SECOND ADVENT OF CHRIST, 237, 258.
  IN HEAVEN, 8, 21, 228, 235, 242, 247, 250.
  MINISTRY OF, 11, 14, 162, 212, 243.
  SONGS OF, 36, 42, 43, 243.
ASHAMED OF JESUS, 121, 186, 203.
ASLEEP IN JESUS—See *Death.*
ASPIRATION:
  FOR CHRIST, 9, 18, 119, 127, 128, 130, 131, 133, 157, 160, 166, 171, 189.
  FOR GOD, 104, 132, 161, 167.
  FOR HEAVEN, 185, 240, 242, 244, 245, 246, 248, 249, 250, 253, 256.
  FOR HOLINESS, 53, 110, 144, 145, 156.
  FOR THE HOLY SPIRIT, 63-71, 156, 230, 238.
  FOR PEACE AND REST, 81, 112, 114, 154, 187, 220, 240, 242, 246.
  OF FAITH—See *Faith.*
  OF HOPE—See *Hope.*
ASSURANCE, 62, 72, 135-139, 142, 165, 172, 174, 182, 185, 188.
ATONEMENT:
  CONSUMMATED, 57, 73, 76, 77, 118, 136, 226.

ATONEMENT:
  DESIRED, 77, 104, 106, 113, 117, 118, 119, 222, 226.
  SUFFICIENT, 74, 83, 85, 88, 93, 226.
ATTRIBUTES OF GOD — See *God.*

BACKSLIDING—See *Declension.*
BAPTISM:
  OF INFANTS, 220, 221.
  OF THE HOLY SPIRIT—See *Holy Spirit.*
BELIEVERS — See *Christians* and *Saints.*
BENEFICENCE, 205, 208, 211.
BEREAVEMENT — See *Affliction.*
BIBLE, 19, 30.
BREAD OF HEAVEN — See *Christ.*
BREVITY OF LIFE—See *Life.*
BROTHERLY LOVE — See *Christian, Fellowship of.*
BURDENS—See *Affliction.*

CALVARY—See *Christ, Crucifixion of.*
CAPTAIN—See *Christ.*
CHARITY—See *Beneficence.*
CHASTENING—See *Affliction.*
CHRIST:
  ABIDING IN US, 7, 8, 9, 10, 17, 18, 225.
  ADORATION OF, 41, 45, 51, 53, 59, 60, 61, 120, 122, 125, 126, 129, 147.
  ADVENT, THE FIRST, 42-47.
  ADVENT OF, THE SECOND, 234, 235, 241, 256, 258.
  ALL IN ALL, 124, 152, 177.
  ASCENSION, 59-61.
  ATONEMENT OF, 55, 73, 76, 77, 85, 101, 111, 113, 114, 118, 119, 120, 126, 136, 226, 228, 229.
  BEAUTY OF, 122, 210, 225, 245.
  BIRTH OF — See *Christ, Advent, The First.*
  BLOOD OF—See *Christ, Crucifixion of.*
  BREAD OF HEAVEN, 163, 175, 176, 182, 190, 194, 195, 200, 250.
  CHARACTER OF, 45, 50-52.
  COMPASSION OF—See *Love of.*
  CONDESCENSION OF—See *Humanity of.*
  CONQUEROR, 41, 57-61, 175.
  CORONATION, 41, 59, 61.
  CROSS OF—See *Cross.*
  CRUCIFIXION OF, 45, 52, 54, 55, 56, 73, 113, 223, 224, 226, 228, 232.
  DEITY OF, 44, 45, 48, 54, 56, 83.
  EXALTATION OF, 46, 59, 60, 61, 234, 235, 237, 247.
  EXAMPLE OF — See *Christ, Character of.*

CHRIST:
  EXCELLENCE OF, 52, 65, 120-123, 125, 126, 129.
  FOUNTAIN, 72, 73, 85, 96, 113, 136, 248.
  FRIEND, 24, 27, 114, 121, 123, 126, 138, 141, 149, 224, 226.
  GLORY OF—See *Christ, Exaltation of.*
  GLORYING IN, 121, 125, 137, 147, 203.
  GRATITUDE TO—See *Gratitude.*
  GUIDE, 24, 91, 99, 160, 161, 182. See also *Guidance.*
  HIGH PRIEST, 54, 62.
  HIDING-PLACE, 27, 111, 113, 117, 189, 225.
  HOPE OF CHRISTIANS — See *Hope.*
  HUMANITY OF, 12, 43-45, 47, 48, 51, 52, 53, 130.
  HUMILIATION OF, 44, 45, 51, 52, 226.
  INTERCESSION OF—See *High Priest.*
  INVITATION OF—See *Invitation.*
  KING OF GLORY—See *Christ, Exaltation of.*
  KNOCKING AT THE DOOR, 98, 101, 115, 118.
  LAMB OF GOD, 51, 53, 54, 73, 77, 107, 119, 222, 225, 233, 245, 246.
  LIFE OF—See *Christ, Character of.*
  LIFE, THE, 49, 72, 123, 129, 137, 141, 231.
  LIGHT, 9, 20-22, 31, 38, 44, 53, 72, 141, 147, 162, 182, 191.
  LONG-SUFFERING OF, 53, 112, 114, 115, 235.
  LORD, 22, 41, 59, 60, 61, 169, 235, 237, 240.
  LOVE OF, 45, 53, 65, 75, 120, 168, 226, 227, 235.
  LOVELINESS OF, 120, 122, 125, 148, 225, 245.
  MAJESTY OF—See *Christ, Deity of,* and *Exaltation of.*
  MAN OF SORROWS—See *Christ, Humiliation of.*
  MASTER, 16, 48, 129, 229.
  MEEKNESS, 44, 45, 51, 53.
  MINISTRY, 12, 48, 51, 53, 130.
  NAME OF, 41, 123, 125, 129, 195, 234.
  NATIVITY OF—See *Christ, Advent of, The First.*
  OFFICES OF—See *Christ, Exaltation of;* also, *High Priest.*
  ONE WITH THE FATHER, 38.
  PASSION—See *Christ, Crucifixion of.*
  PASSOVER, 222.
  PATIENCE—See *Christ, Long-suffering of.*
  PATTERN—See *Christ, Character of.*

INDEX OF SUBJECTS.

CHRIST:
  PHYSICIAN—See *Sickness.*
  PILOT, 95, 169, 171.
  PRECIOUS, 120-123, 125, 126, 129, 148, 170.
  REIGNING—See *Christ, Exaltation of.*
  RESURRECTION OF, 57, 58, 62, 230.
  ROCK OF AGES, 37, 113, 216, 248.
  SACRIFICE—See *Christ, Crucifixion of,* and *Atonement of.*
  SAVIOUR, 35, 76, 78, 82, 83, 112, 114, 119, 126, 157, 160.
  SECOND COMING—See *Christ, Advent of, The Second.*
  SHEPHERD, 89, 96, 142, 157, 165, 231, 235, 243.
  SON OF GOD, 29, 54, 236.
  SUN OF RIGHTEOUSNESS, 8, 9, 20, 31, 38, 253.
  SYMPATHY OF, 7, 12, 48, 50, 53, 140.
  TEMPTATION OF, 12, 45, 51.
  UNION WITH—See *Saints.*
  UNSEEN, 38, 148, 149.
  WAY, TRUTH AND LIFE, THE, 49, 231.
CHRISTIAN ACTIVITY—See *Christians, Activity of.*
CHRISTIANS:
  ACTIVITY OF, 192-210, 261.
  ASPIRATION OF—See *Aspiration.*
  BLESSEDNESS OF, 4, 153, 154, 165, 172, 174.
  CHRIST, THE LIFE OF—See *Christ, the Life.*
  CONFLICT OF, 27, 96, 140, 145, 150, 155-157, 175, 177, 179, 182, 186, 187, 189, 230.
  CONQUERORS BY GRACE, 180, 182, 183, 185, 212, 250.
  DUTIES OF, 91, 181, 192, 196, 199, 200, 201, 204, 205.
  ENCOURAGEMENTS OF, 139, 142, 165, 172, 174, 176-178, 185.
  EXAMPLE OF, 192, 196, 204.
  FELLOWSHIP OF, 15, 28, 163, 172, 214, 215, 219.
  FOLLOWING CHRIST, 50, 51, 102, 130, 152, 157, 158, 160, 164, 168, 173, 174, 193, 194, 217. See also *Guidance.*
  GRACES OF, 128, 135, 140, 144, 151, 152, 158, 178, 204. See also *Faith, Hope* and *Love.*
  SYMPATHY OF—See *Christians, Fellowship of.*
CHRISTIAN ENDEAVOR WORK:
  ACTIVITY, 182, 194-197, 200, 261.
  BENEDICTION, 17, 212.
  CONSECRATION — See *Consecration.*
  RECEPTION OF MEMBERS, 213.
CHRISTMAS—See *Christ, First Advent of.*
CHURCH:
  AFFLICTED, 175, 217.
  CHILDREN OF THE, 11, 220, 221.

CHURCH:
  FUTURE OF THE, 15, 216, 218, 234, 240.
  GROWTH OF THE—See *Missions* and *Kingdom of Christ.*
  LOVE FOR THE, 214, 215.
  MILITANT—See *Warfare.*
  SACRAMENTS OF THE — See *Baptism* and *Lord's Supper.*
  STABILITY OF THE, 163, 214, 216, 218.
  TRIUMPH OF THE—See *Kingdom of Christ.*
  UNITY OF THE, 15, 163, 194, 195, 213, 215, 217, 219.
CITY OF GOD—See *Heaven* and *Kingdom of Christ.*
CLOSE OF SERVICE, 6, 11, 13, 14, 16-22, 212.
COMFORT—See *Affliction.*
COMFORTER—See *Holy Spirit.*
COMING TO CHRIST — See *Sinners.*
COMMUNION—See also *Lord's Supper.*
  OF SAINTS—See *Christians, Fellowship of.*
  WITH GOD, 6, 10, 26, 131, 132, 145.
  WITH JESUS, 23, 27, 131, 134, 149, 224, 227, 228.
CONFESSION:
  OF CHRIST—See *Sinners.*
  OF FAITH—See *Faith.*
  OF SIN—See *Sin.*
CONFIDENCE, 62, 110, 137, 139, 140, 142, 165, 174.
CONFLICT—See *Christian, Conflict of.*
CONSECRATION:
  OF POSSESSIONS, 56, 109, 208, 211, 229.
  OF SELF, 13, 55, 70, 99, 103, 104, 109, 200, 210, 211, 229.
CONSOLATION—See *Affliction.*
CONSTANCY, 52, 174, 176-183, 185-187, 190.
CONTENTMENT, 140, 142, 144, 149, 153, 154, 165, 174, 191.
CONTRITION—See *Repentance* and *Sinners.*
CONVERSION — See *Sinners, Repentant* and *Faith.*
COURAGE, 163, 174-177, 179, 180, 182, 184-186, 190, 194.
COVENANT, ENTERING INTO, 55, 56, 104, 109, 211, 229, 231.
CROSS:
  AT THE CROSS — See *Christ, Crucifixion of.*
  BANNER OF THE, 17, 163, 194, 195, 207, 210, 216.
  BEARING THE, 50, 103, 175, 186, 188, 203, 261.
  GLORYING IN, 50, 103, 147, 186, 188, 207.
  SOLDIERS OF, 163, 182, 186, 190, 194, 195.
CROWN OF GLORY, 176, 179, 180, 183, 185, 188, 190, 199, 212, 250, 251, 253.
CRUCIFIXION—See also *Christ* To the World, 56, 103.

DARKNESS, SPIRITUAL—See *Christians, Conflict of.*
DAY OF GRACE—See *Accepted Time* and *Invitation.*
DEATH, 5, 7, 14, 16-18, 20, 25, 90, 128, 132, 148, 166, 219, 226, 239, 243, 257.
DECLENSION, SPIRITUAL, 63, 67, 115, 145.
DEPENDENCE ON CHRIST—See *Trust.*
DESPONDENCE — See *Christians, Conflict of.*
DISMISSION—See *Close of Service.*
DOUBT—See *Christians, Conflict of.*

EARLY PIETY—See *Children.*
EASTER—See *Christ, Resurrection of.*
ETERNAL LIFE—See *Heaven.*
ETERNITY, 32, 36, 37, 87, 126, 142, 194, 244, 245, 248, 250, 251, 257.
EVENING, 3, 5-22, 25, 26.
EXAMPLE:
  OF CHRIST—See *Christ.*
  OF CHRISTIANS — See *Christians.*

FAITH:
  ACT OF—See *Sinners.*
  ASPIRATION OF—See *Aspiration.*
  BLESSEDNESS OF, 72, 128, 136, 138, 140, 141, 149.
  CONFESSION OF, 103, 109, 110, 118, 119, 121, 137.
  JUSTIFICATION BY, 76, 77, 111, 113, 118, 137, 164.
  WALKING BY, 164, 174, 178, 187, 240.
FATHERHOOD OF GOD—See *God.*
FOLLOWING CHRIST — See *Christ.*
FORGIVENESS OF SIN — See *Sinners.*
FORSAKING ALL FOR CHRIST—See *Consecration.*
FOUNTAIN—See *Christ.*
FRAILTY OF MAN—See *Life.*
FUTURE PUNISHMENT—See *Life.*

GOD:
  ADORATION OF, 1, 15, 21, 32-37, 39, 40.
  ALL IN ALL, 21, 22, 152.
  ALMIGHTY, 1, 2, 33, 36, 39, 40, 169.
  ATTRIBUTES OF, 1, 33, 34, 40.
  COMMUNION WITH—See *Communion.*
  CONDESCENSION OF, 33, 39, 74, 76.
  CREATOR, 37, 39, 40, 78, 165, 255.
  DWELLING-PLACE, OUR, 19, 37, 111, 142.
  ETERNAL, 32, 36, 37.
  FAITHFUL, 34, 39, 134, 138, 139.
  FATHER, 2, 36, 104, 106, 143.
  FORBEARANCE OF — See *Patience of.*

INDEX OF SUBJECTS.

GOD:
  GLORY OF, 31, 36, 40.
  GOODNESS OF—See *Love of*.
  GRACE OF, 33, 35, 76, 128, 139, 143.
  GUIDE, 106, 152, 161, 166, 167, 220.
  HOLINESS OF, 1, 33, 36.
  IMMUTABLE — See *Unchangeable*.
  INCOMPREHENSIBLE, 150.
  INFINITE—See *Eternal*.
  LONG-SUFFERING OF—See *Patience of*.
  LOVE OF, 13, 31, 33, 34, 39, 40, 74, 142, 153.
  MAJESTY OF, 1, 31, 33, 36, 40.
  MERCY OF, 19, 34, 35, 74.
  OMNIPOTENT—See *Almighty*.
  OMNIPRESENT, 36, 138.
  PATIENCE OF, 108.
  PRAISE OF—See *Praise*.
  PROVIDENCE OF, 40, 138, 142, 150, 153, 258.
  REFUGE, 32, 37.
  REIGN OF, 15, 36, 39.
  SUPREME, 2, 39.
  SYMPATHY OF, 7.
  TRIUNE, 1, 2, 19.
  UNCHANGEABLE, 32, 37.
  WISDOM OF, 33, 34, 165.
GOSPEL:
  BANNER—See *Cross*.
  EXCELLENCE OF, 29, 30, 76.
  FREENESS OF, 74, 83, 85, 88, 92.
  FULNESS OF, 74, 76.
  INVITATION OF—See *Invitation*.
  SPREAD OF—See *Missions*.
GRACE—See also *God*.
  MAGNIFIED, 4, 35, 72, 136, 137, 224.
  REVIVING—See *Holy Spirit*.
  SANCTIFYING—See *Holy Spirit*.
  WIDENESS OF, 29, 74, 76, 83, 92.
GRACES, CHRISTIAN — See *Faith, Hope, Love* and *Peace*.
GRATITUDE, 35, 55, 56, 226.
GROWTH, CHRISTIAN, 10, 51, 132, 133, 144, 204, 258.
GUIDANCE:
  ENJOYED, 142, 164, 165, 174, 178, 182, 194, 200, 216, 217.
  SOUGHT, 7, 22, 63, 152, 157, 158, 160-162, 164, 166, 167, 171, 173, 210, 213, 220, 231.
GUILT—See *Sin*.

HAPPINESS—See *Joy*.
HARVEST, 193, 209, 256, 258.
HEART:
  CHANGE OF—See *Regeneration*.
  CONTRITE, 55, 104, 107, 109, 112, 114, 117.
  PURE, 64, 69, 144, 253.
  SINFUL—See *Sin*.
  SURRENDER OF, 55, 89, 99, 104, 106, 108, 124, 229.
HEALING—See *Sickness*.
HEAVEN:
  ANTICIPATED, 26, 65, 76, 131, 135, 136, 137, 140, 146, 150, 160, 172, 174, 187, 239, 241, 246.
  BLESSEDNESS OF, 242, 245-251, 256.
  DESIRED, 240, 242, 244, 246-249, 252, 253.

HEAVEN:
  HOME, 32, 88, 159, 242, 245, 248, 250.
  REST OF, 146, 246, 251, 256.
  SOCIETY OF, 159, 241, 242, 245, 250, 251.
  SONGS OF, 21, 22, 187, 235, 242, 243, 247, 250, 253.
HEIRSHIP—See *Adoption*.
HOLINESS—See *God, Heaven* and *Saints*.
HOLY SCRIPTURES — See *Bible*.
HOLY SPIRIT:
  BAPTISM OF, 66, 68, 69, 70, 71, 238.
  COMFORTER, 65, 156.
  DEITY OF, 2, 66.
  DESCENT OF, 66, 68, 69, 70, 71, 167.
  ENLIGHTENER, 37, 64, 69, 156, 230.
  GUIDE, 111, 156, 167, 210.
  INDWELLING OF, 143, 210.
  INFILLING OF, 65, 66, 70, 71, 167.
  INSPIRING, 30, 68, 70, 71, 198.
  REGENERATING, 64, 116, 144, 156, 238.
  SANCTIFYING, 64, 69, 70, 156.
  SOUGHT, 2, 19, 63, 67-70, 116, 145, 238.
  STRIVING, 78, 79, 108.
  TEACHER OF PRAYER, 65, 116.
  WITNESS OF, 2, 156.
HOME MISSIONS—See *Missions*.
HOPE:
  IN AFFLICTION—See *Affliction*.
  IN CHRIST, 62, 118, 136, 137, 147, 182, 189.
  IN GOD, 37, 143, 172.
  OF HEAVEN—See *Heaven*.
HUMILITY, 107, 112, 114, 117, 118, 128, 144, 164, 168.

IMMORTALITY—See *Heaven*.
IMPORTUNITY—See *Prayer*.
IMPUTATION—See *Atonement*.
INCARNATION—See *Christ*.
INSPIRATION—See *Bible* and *Holy Spirit*.
INTERCESSION—See *Christ*.
INVITATION, 79-99, 101, 105, 108, 243.
INVOCATION, 2, 8, 35, 38.

JERUSALEM, THE NEW—See *Heaven*.
JESUS—See *Christ*.
JOY, 4, 46, 72, 103, 125, 128-130, 137, 141, 147, 172, 174, 196.
JUDGMENT, 90, 192, 257, 258.
JUSTICE OF GOD—See *God*.
JUSTIFICATION—See *Faith*.

KINGDOM OF CHRIST:
  PRAYER FOR, 65, 85, 214, 238.
  PROGRESS OF, 15, 46, 218, 234-237, 261.
  TRIUMPH OF, 15, 42, 85, 94, 200, 216, 235, 237.

LAMB OF GOD—See *Christ*.
LAW OF GOD, 51, 92, 232, 235.
LIBERTY, 195, 259.
LIFE:
  BREVITY OF, 3, 5, 14, 18, 22, 32, 37, 87, 90, 193, 209, 251.

LIFE:
  CHRIST, THE LIFE—See *Christ*.
  OBJECT OF, 3, 180, 181.
  SOLEMNITY OF, 80, 87, 90, 95, 179, 181, 193, 257, 258.
  VANITY OF, 22, 32, 37.
LIGHT—See *Christ, Guidance* and *Evening*.
LONGINGS—See *Aspiration*.
LOOKING TO JESUS, 72, 112, 119.
LORD'S DAY, THE—See *Evening*.
LORD'S SUPPER, THE, 45, 52-56, 222-230, 232.
LOVE:
  BANNER OF, 17, 194, 210, 227, 230.
  BROTHERLY, 163, 194, 195, 215, 217.
  FOR CHRIST, 48, 53, 99, 105, 123, 125, 126, 133, 148, 168, 189.
  FOR GOD, 4, 33.
  FOR THE CHURCH, 214, 215.
  OF CHRIST—See *Christ*.
  OF GOD—See *God*.

MANNA—See *Christ, the Bread*.
MARINERS—See *Sea, Those at*.
MARTYRS, 36, 175.
MEDITATION, 6, 26, 224.
MEEKNESS, 16, 50, 51.
MERCY—See *God* and *Sinners*.
MERCY-SEAT, 23.
MINISTRY, 29, 192, 194, 195, 197, 198, 199, 200, 207, 210, 212, 238.
MISSIONS—See also *Kingdom of Christ*.
  FOREIGN, 15, 195, 207, 233-238.
  HOME, 193-195, 197-200, 206, 235, 261.
MORNING, 1, 3, 6, 9, 13, 26.
MORTALITY—See *Life*.

NATIONAL, 254, 259, 260, 262.
NATIVITY OF CHRIST—See *Christ*.
NATURE, 15, 19, 31, 37, 40, 174, 255, 259.
NEARNESS TO GOD, 6, 18, 20, 53, 132, 145, 158, 165.
NEW JERUSALEM—See *Heaven*.
NEW YEAR, 32, 255, 257.
NIGHT—See *Evening*.
NOW—See *Accepted Time*.

OBEDIENCE, 152, 164, 168.
OFFERINGS—See *Beneficence*.
OLD AGE, 18, 139, 201.
OMNIPOTENCE—See *God*.
OMNIPRESENCE—See *God*.
OPENING OF SERVICE—See *Invocation, Evening* and *Morning*.
ORDINANCES — See *Baptism* and *Lord's Supper*.
ORIGINAL SIN—See *Sin*.

PARADISE—See *Heaven*.
PARDON:
  FOUND—See *Sinners*.
  OFFERED—See *Invitation*.
  SOUGHT—See *Sinners*.

INDEX OF SUBJECTS. 163

PARTING—See *Close of Service.*
PASSOVER—See *Christ.*
PASTORS—See *Ministry.*
PATIENCE—See *Affliction, Christ* and *God.*
PATTERN—See *Christ.*
PEACE:
   For the Inquirer, 42, 77, 83, 105.
   Of the Christian, 14, 26, 29, 42, 129, 134, 135, 141, 147, 153, 154, 165, 167.
   Sought, 25, 154, 156.
PENITENCE—See *Repentance.*
PENTECOST, 66, 68, 69, 71.
PERSEVERANCE—See *Saints.*
PILGRIMAGE, 4, 159, 161, 162, 165, 166, 172, 174, 178, 187, 217, 220, 240, 243, 246.
PRAISE:
   Of the Father, 10, 14, 21, 25, 31, 32, 33, 35, 36, 37, 39, 76, 140, 153, 154, 255.
   Of the Son, 4, 25, 35, 38, 41, 45, 46, 50, 53, 60, 61, 125, 126, 129, 136, 137, 141, 235.
   Of the Trinity, 1, 2, 4, 13, 15, 31-34, 36, 37, 39, 40, 255, 259.
PRAYER—See also *Invocation* and *Mercy-seat.*
   Exhortation to, 24, 27, 28, 179, 180, 182, 184, 190, 227.
   Hour of, 6, 7, 10, 26.
   Revival through, 28, 67.
   To the Father—See *God.*
   To the Holy Spirit—See *Holy Spirit.*
   To the Son—See *Christ.*
PROBATION—See *Accepted Time* and *Life.*
PROCRASTINATION—See *Accepted Time* and *Life.*
PROGRESS, CHRISTIAN—See *Growth.*
PROMISED LAND—See *Heaven.*
PROMISES, 92, 109, 114, 117, 118, 134, 139.
PROVIDENCE—See *God.*
PURE IN HEART—See *Heart.*

RACE, CHRISTIAN, 176-178, 185.
REDEMPTION—See *Atonement.*
REFUGE—See *Christ* and *God.*
REGENERATION—See *Holy Spirit.*
REJOICING IN GOD—See *Joy.*
REMEMBRANCE OF CHRIST—See *Lord's Supper.*
RENOUNCING ALL FOR CHRIST—See *Consecration.*
REPENTANCE, 54, 55, 100, 104, 107, 109, 112-114, 116-118, 210, 226, 229.
RESIGNATION—See *Affliction.*
REST:
   Physical, 7, 11, 19, 20.
   Spiritual—See *Heaven* and *Weary.*
RESURRECTION:
   Of Christ—See *Christ.*
   Of Christians, 14, 57, 137, 251, 258.
REVELATION—See *Bible.*

REVIVAL:
   Rejoicing in, 235.
   Sought, 28, 63-71, 145, 238.
RICHES, 56, 59, 140, 213.
ROCK OF AGES—See *Christ.*

SABBATH—See *Evening.*
SACRAMENTS—See *Baptism* and *Lord's Supper.*
SACRIFICE—See *Atonement* and *Christ.*
SAFETY OF CHRISTIANS—See *Saints.*
SAILORS—See *Sea.*
SAINTS:
   Blessedness of—See *Christians.*
   Communion of—See *Love.*
   Death of, 140, 141, 239. See also *Life.*
   Glorified, 22, 242, 245, 249, 250.
   Perseverance of, 137, 139, 172, 176, 179, 180, 182, 183, 188, 190, 194, 196, 203, 210, 212.
   Security of, 32, 134, 137, 139, 142, 165, 169, 182.
   Union with, 120, 144, 149, 165, 170, 225.
   Unity of, 163, 194, 215, 217, 219.
SATAN, 76, 174, 179, 180, 182, 184.
SAVIOUR—See *Christ.*
SCRIPTURES, HOLY—See *Bible.*
SEA, THOSE AT, 11, 95, 105, 138, 169, 171.
SEASONS, 255, 257, 258.
SECOND BIRTH—See *Holy Spirit.*
SECOND COMING—See *Christ.*
SECOND DEATH—See *Life.*
SECURITY OF SAINTS—See *Saints.*
SELF-DEDICATION—See *Consecration* and *Covenant.*
SELF-DENIAL, 50, 103, 186, 188, 203.
SHEPHERD—See *Christ.*
SICKNESS, 12, 222, 261.
SIN:
   Confession of, 10, 12, 16, 102, 104, 106, 112-115, 117, 118. See also *Repentance.*
   Hatred of, 55, 136, 145, 189.
   Indwelling, 12, 76, 114, 129.
SINNERS:
   Anxious, 29, 86, 92, 97.
   Awakened, 81, 98, 108.
   Believing, 77, 103, 107, 109, 119.
   Careless, 3, 78, 87, 93, 108, 115.
   Coming to Christ, 72, 102, 104, 106, 107, 109-112, 114, 117, 118, 124.
   Confession of Christ, 120-123, 136, 137.
   Invited—See *Invitation.*
   Penitent—See *Repentance.*
   Pleading for Pardon, 5, 10, 13, 100, 104, 109, 112-114, 119, 124, 189.
   Warned, 3, 80, 82, 87, 90, 91, 93, 95, 192.
SLEEP, 7, 11, 13, 14, 20.
SOLDIER, CHRISTIAN—See *Warfare.*
SON OF GOD—See *Christ.*

SORROW—See *Affliction* and *Repentance.*
SOWING AND REAPING—See *Harvest.*
STAR OF THE EAST, 38, 47.
STEADFASTNESS—See *Saints.*
SUBMISSION—See *Affliction.*
SUFFERING—See *Affliction.*
SUPPER, THE LORD'S—See *Lord's Supper.*
SURRENDER—See *Sinners.*
SYMPATHY—See *Christ* and *Christians.*

TEMPTATION, 16, 53, 112, 161, 176, 179, 180, 182-184.
THANKFULNESS—See *Gratitude.*
THANKSGIVING, 35, 129, 136, 153, 154, 235, 258, 259.
THRONE OF GRACE—See *Mercy-seat.*
TIME—See *Life* and *Year.*
TOIL—See *Labor.*
TRIALS—See *Affliction.*
TRIBULATION—See *Affliction.*
TRINITY—See *Christ, God, Holy Spirit, Praise* and *Prayer.*
TRUST:
   In Christ, 62, 109, 110, 118, 120, 134, 135, 149, 151, 165.
   In God, 7, 13, 14, 32, 142, 150.
   In Providence, 139, 150.
TRUTH, 29-31, 39.

VANITY OF LIFE—See *Life.*
VICTORY OF BELIEVERS—See *Warfare.*
VICTORY OF CHRIST—See *Christ.*
VOWS TO GOD, 220, 229, 231.

WAITING ON GOD, 26, 70, 131, 144, 228.
WALKING:
   With Christ, 38, 149, 158, 165.
   With God, 142, 145.
WARFARE, 94, 163, 175-177, 179-187, 190, 194, 195, 200, 212, 213.
WARNING—See *Sinners.*
WATCHFULNESS, 179, 181, 184.
WAY OF SALVATION—See *Atonement, Grace* and *Sinners.*
WAY, TRUTH AND LIFE—See *Christ.*
WEARY, REST FOR THE, 12, 72, 81, 91, 97, 98, 134, 141, 243.
WITNESSES, THE CLOUD OF, 175, 182, 185.
WORD OF GOD—See *Bible.*
WORK—See *Christians, Activity of.*
WORLD RENOUNCED—See *Consecration.*
WORSHIP—See *Lord's Day, Praise* and *Prayer.*

YEAR, 32, 37, 255, 257.
YIELDING TO CHRIST—See *Sinners* and *Repentance.*

ZEAL—See *Christians, Activity of,* and *Warfare.*
ZION—See *Church.*

INDEX OF FIRST LINES.

A charge to keep I have	181
Abide with me: fast falls the eventide	18
According to Thy gracious word	223
After the heat of the summer sun	256
Alas! and did my Saviour bleed	55
All hail the power of Jesus' name	41
Along the highway of the King	174
Am I a soldier of the Cross	186
Art thou weary, art thou languid	97
As with gladness men of old	47
Ask ye what great thing I know	137
At even, ere the sun was set	12
Awake, my soul, stretch every nerve	185
Before Jehovah's awful throne	39
Behold, what wondrous grace	143
Blessèd fountain, full of grace	136
Blest be the tie that binds	215
Brief life is here our portion	251
Brother, hast thou wandered far	86
Brother, sailing o'er life's ocean	95
Brothers, we are marching on	194
By cool Siloam's shady rill	221
Children of the heavenly King	172
Christ, above all glory seated	60
Christ, for sinners crucified	118
Christ for the world, we sing	261
Christ, the Lord, is risen to-day	57
Christ, throughout the ages waging	94
Christ, whose glory fills the skies	9
Christian, seek not yet repose	184
Come, Holy Spirit, come	64
Come, Holy Spirit, heavenly Dove	63
Come, Thou almighty King	2
Come, Thou Fount of every blessing	35
Come, thou weary, Jesus calls thee	98
Come, my soul, thy suit prepare	24
Come, we that love the Lord	4
Come with your sins to Jesus	96
Come, ye thankful people, come	258
Come ye yourselves apart in desert places	228
Daily, daily sing the praises	247
Down from their home on high	58
Draw near, O Holy Dove, draw near	230
Far out on the desolate billow	138
Fight the good fight with all thy might	177
Fling out the banner, let it float	207
For thee, O dear, dear Country	248
Forward, host of Heaven	195
From every stormy wind that blows	23
From Greenland's icy mountains	233
Gently falls the even	16
Glorious things of thee are spoken	216
Go forward, Christian soldier	182
Go, labor on; spend and be spent	201
Go, labor on while it is day	199
Go ye forth the word to carry	197
God be with you till we meet again	17
God bless our native land	260
God calling yet, shall I not hear	108
God, in the gospel of His Son	29
God is love; His mercy brightens	34
God loved the world of sinners lost	76
God moves in a mysterious way	150
God of my life, Thy boundless grace	111
Guide me, O Thou great Jehovah	166
Hail to the Lord's Anointed	234
Hark, hark, my soul, angelic songs	243
Hark, it is the angelus	7
Hark, the Shepherd's voice is calling	89
Hark! the voice of Jesus calling	105
Hark, the voice of the Lord Jesus calling	91
He that goeth forth with weeping	202
Holy Ghost, the Infinite	156
Holy, Holy, Holy! Lord God Almighty	1
How firm a foundation, ye saints of the Lord	139
How shall I follow Him I serve	52
How sweet the name of Jesus sounds	123
I am coming to the cross	109
I am trusting Thee, Lord Jesus	110
I heard the voice of Jesus say	72
I know that my Redeemer lives	62
I love Thy Kingdom, Lord	214
I love to tell the story	75
I'm but a stranger here	159
In heavenly love abiding	165
In the cross of Christ I glory	147
In the dark and cloudy day	155
It came upon the midnight clear	42

INDEX OF FIRST LINES.

Jerusalem, the glorious	249
Jerusalem, the golden	250
Jesus, and shall it ever be	121
Jesus calls us o'er the tumult	99
Jesus, I my cross have taken	103
Jesus is calling to you	101
Jesus, Lord, I turn to Thee	112
Jesus, Lover of my soul	189
Jesus, my Lord, how oft I long	130
"Jesus only!" In the shadow	170
Jesus, Saviour, be my guide	160
Jesus, Saviour, pilot me	171
Jesus, Saviour, sick of sin	114
Jesus, Saviour, Thou hast sought me	157
Jesus shall reign where'er the sun	237
Jesus, the very thought of Thee	125
Jesus, these eyes have never seen	148
Joy to the world, the Lord is come	46
Just as I am, without one plea	107
Laboring and heavy laden	100
Lead, kindly Light, amid the encircling	162
Lead us, Heavenly Father, lead us	167
Let saints below in concert sing	219
Let the light that is in you be shining	196
Look, ye saints, the sight is glorious	61
Lord, as to Thy dear cross we flee	50
Lord God, the Holy Ghost	66
Lord, I am Thine, entirely Thine	229
Lord of all being, throned afar	31
Lord, speak to me, that I may speak	198
Lord, Thy children guide and keep	161
Love divine, all loves excelling	65
Majestic sweetness sits enthroned	122
Master, the tempest is raging	169
May the God of peace watch o'er you	212
Mine eyes have seen the glory of the	262
Mine to follow, Thine to lead	164
More love to Thee, O Christ	133
Morning calls, bright shining o'er thee	3
Must Jesus bear the cross alone	188
My country, 'tis of thee	259
My dear Redeemer and my Lord	51
My faith looks up to Thee	119
My feet are weary with the march	240
My God, accept my heart this day	124
My God, how endless is Thy love	13
My God, how wonderful Thou art	33
My God, is any hour so sweet	26
My Jesus, as Thou wilt	151
My soul, be on thy guard	179
My soul, weigh not thy life	180
Nearer, my God, to Thee	132
Night of wonder; night of glory	44
None but Christ: His merit hides me	120
Not all the blood of beasts	77
Now from labor and from care	10
Now is the accepted time	80
Now the day is over	11
O cease, my wandering soul	81
O could I speak the matchless worth	126
O do not let the word depart	93
O for a closer walk with God	145
O for a heart to praise my God	144
O for a thousand tongues to sing	129
O gift of gifts, oh, grace of faith	128
O God, beneath Thy guiding hand	254
O God of Bethel, by whose hand	220
O God, the Rock of ages	37
O God, we praise Thee, and confess	36
O God, who flamed on Horeb's hill	68
O Holy One, in earth's creation	70
O Holy Saviour, Friend unseen	149
O Jesus, Thou art standing	115
O Lamb of God! O Lamb of God	53
O Lamb of God, still keep me	225
O Lord, Thy work revive	67
O Love divine, who seekest	235
O One with God the Father	38
O Paradise! O Paradise	244
O pray ye for others: the showers	28
O radiant City! O City of song	245
O sacred Head, now wounded	226
O Spirit of the living God	238
O sweet and blessed Country	252
O the lights are ever shining	88
O Thou, the eternal Son of God	54
O Thou whose bounty fills my cup	153
O where are kings and empires now	218
O worship the King; all glorious above	40
Of all the thoughts which days of old	134
Of all the words of Christ, our Lord	92
On this eve of consecration	210
Once more the feast of love is spread	222
One sweetly solemn thought	239
Only a step to Jesus	84
Only a voice in the desert of sin	192
Onward, Christian soldiers	163
Our day of praise is done	21
Our God, our help in ages past	32
Out of my darkness into Thy light	102
Peace, perfect peace in this dark world	135

Rest of the weary	141
Rock of Ages, cleft for me	113
Saviour, again to Thy dear Name we raise	25
Saviour, for refuge	117
Saviour, I follow on	158
Saviour, lead me lest I stray	173
Saviour teach me day by day	168
Scorn not the slightest word or deed	205
See, yonder stands the wheat unbroken	206
Sing of His love who descended	45
Sinners, turn, why will ye die	78
Sit down beneath His shadow	227
So let our lips and lives express	204
Soft, as they list, the airs of heaven	116
Softly now the light of day	5
Softly the twilight fades	19
Sometimes a light surprises	191
Spirit divine, attend our prayers	69
Spirit divine, who once descended	71
Stand up, my soul, shake off thy fears	176
Stand up, stand up for Jesus	190
Still, still with Thee, my God	6
Sun of my soul, Thou Saviour dear	20
Sweet the moments, rich in blessing	224
Take me, O my Father, take me	104
Take my heart, O Father! take it	106
Take my life, and let it be	211
Take up thy cross, the Saviour said	203
Talk with me, Lord, Thyself reveal	131
The day, O Lord, is spent	8
The day Thou gavest, Lord, is ended	15
The harvest dawn is near	209
The Head that once was crowned with thorns	59
The Homeland! O the Homeland	242
The Lord's my Shepherd, I'll not want	142
The message here is spoken	90
The morning light is breaking	236
The people of the Lord	187
The radiant morn hath passed away	22
The roseate hues of early dawn	253
The Son of God goes forth to war	175
The Spirit breathes upon the word	30
The Spirit in our heart	79
The voice of Christ, the Saviour	83
There is a fountain filled with blood	73
There is a fountain flowing	85
There's a wideness in God's mercy	74
Thine forever; God of love	231
This is not my place for resting	246
Thou art the Way: to Thee alone	49
Thou who roll'st the year around	257
Thrice the Master hastened	193
Through the conflict of the ages	200
Through the night of doubt and sorrow	217
Thus far the Lord has led me on	14
Thy way, not mine, O Lord	152
To-day the Saviour calls	82
Time is earnest, passing by	87
'Tis by the faith of joys to come	178
We bless Thee for Thy peace, O God	154
We give Thee but Thine own	208
We may not climb the heavenly steeps	48
We stand to bid you welcome	213
We would see Jesus, for the shadows lengthen	127
What a friend we have in Jesus	27
What fulness of possession	140
When I can read my title clear	146
When I gaze on the silvery splendor	255
When I survey the wondrous cross	56
When on Sinai's top I see	232
When the trumpet of the Lord shall sound	241
While shepherds watched their flocks	43
Yield not to temptation	183

www.ingramcontent.com/pod-product-compliance
Lightning Source LLC
Chambersburg PA
CBHW030246170426
43202CB00009B/648